The Black Hills
Yesterday & Today

By Paul Horsted

Design By Camille Riner

Author's Note

Most of the images in this book are available as art prints suitable for framing. Please visit www.dakotaphoto.com for details.

I am available as a speaker on subjects relating to the Black Hills, its history and photography. I am also interested in any collections of historic photos of the Black Hills, South Dakota and eastern Wyoming. Email is the most efficient way to contact me, or you may write to the address below.

Paul Horsted
horsted@dakotaphoto.com

Dakota Photographic LLC
24905 Mica Ridge Road
Custer, SD 57730

Other books by Paul Horsted, available at www.dakotaphoto.com, or at your favorite bookstore:

Exploring With Custer: The 1874 Black Hills Expedition
(co-authored with Ernest Grafe) A uniquely intimate portrait of this fascinating Expedition emerges from the first photographs ever taken in the Black Hills, carefully matched with present-day images, and excerpts from every known firsthand account. The experience of the trail comes alive in the blend of photographs with personal diaries, newspaper stories and official reports. Maps and GPS coordinates also pinpoint dozens of locations visited, described or photographed in 1874. More information at www.custertrail.com.

Custer State Park: From the Mountains to the Plains
Custer State Park's 71,000 acres encompass a vast landscape of towering granite peaks, pine-covered mountains, sparkling lakes, and flower-strewn prairies. The Park is home to abundant wildlife, including one of the world's largest bison herds, and its natural beauty attracts more than a million visitors each year. Join photographer Paul Horsted on a scenic tour of this "Jewel of the Black Hills" as you explore Custer State Park through stunning nature photographs created over a period of nearly 20 years. Samples from the book at www.dakotaphoto.com.

The Black Hills Yesterday & Today is published by Golden Valley Press, an imprint of Dakota Photographic LLC, Custer, South Dakota, 57730.

©2006 by Dakota Photographic LLC, All Rights Reserved. No part of this publication may be reproduced or transmitted in any form or by any means now known or hereafter invented, electronic or mechanical, including photocopy, recording, or any information storage, online or retrieval system, without permission in writing from the publisher. Photographs (if not otherwise credited) and related text are ©Paul Horsted.

The information contained in this book is accurate to the best of the author's knowledge. The author and publisher assume no liability whatsoever for errors or omissions of any kind. Boundaries and land ownership change often in the Black Hills; please check with local offices of the U.S. Forest Service or county planning agencies for the latest maps and information. This book may depict areas that are privately owned; such depiction does not mean these areas are open to the public. Always obtain permission from the owner before entering or crossing any private property.

FIRST EDITION: October 2006.

ISBN-13: 978-0-9718053-3-0
ISBN-10: 0-9718053-3-4
Library of Congress Control Number: 2006925298

Designer: Camille Riner.
Editor: Ernest Grafe.
Research Consultant: David Wolff, Ph.D.
Produced and published in the United States of America. Printed in the Republic of Korea by Doosan Printing.

See page 301 for a complete list of sources and collections which provided material for this book.

(Left) Spearfish Falls (Adams Museum & House/Locke & McBride)
(Facing page) Unidentified 1870s photographer (Minnilusa Pioneer Museum/Bishop)

The following is a list of photographers whose work appears in this book. It was my great pleasure to follow in their footsteps, and to them this book is gratefully dedicated.

William C. Allison	Eastman	Lease	Pollock & Boyden
A.L. Bishop	Justus Fey	Locke & McBride	Pollock & Duganne
Butcher & Son	J.C.H. Grabill	Locke & Peterson	Quiggle & Johnson
C.C. McBride	A. (or Fritz W.) Guerin	Loock (Rise Studio)	Quigley Studio
Canedy	B.E. Hawkins	C.B. Manville	Carl Rise
Clarke	F. Jay Haynes	L.W. Marble	Specialty Photographic Co.
William J. Collins	Hollister	T.H. Mayberry	Stevens
Coules & McBride	William Henry Illingworth	Stanley J. Morrow	C.W. Stiff
William Richard Cross	William Henry Jackson	O'Neill Photo Co.	*And for the many who did not add their names to their work,*
Charles D'emery	J. Harlan Johnson	W.B. Perkins	
Lewis Darrow	Kirch (Rise Studio)	J.W. Pike	Photographer Unknown

Preservation of Historic Photographs

Photographs of the early days of the Black Hills, like those reproduced in this book, are a priceless link to our past. If you own such images, I encourage you to take time now to insure they are preserved for future generations. Consider that Black Hills photos in your grandfather's personal album could be just as interesting for historical purposes as those taken by well-known studio photographers. They were probably the only prints of those images ever made, meaning that most amateur photos truly are "one of a kind." They should be cared for accordingly.

Antique prints, stereoviews and even glass plate negatives can be digitally scanned in a simple process that does no harm to the original and will preserve the image should the original ever fade or be lost. If you have any questions about this subject, feel free to contact the author; information is provided on the opposite page.

Consider donating your originals to one of the many museums or archives listed on page 301. This is the best way to insure that the images can be studied and preserved for future historical purposes.

Inquiries about historic photos of the greater Black Hills region and South Dakota are welcome; we hope to pursue future projects to showcase more of these fascinating images.

—P.H.

Sylvan Lake Lodge. (Adams Museum & House/Locke)

Table of Contents

	Dedication to photographers	3
	Preface	6
	Introduction	9
	Key to the photographs	11
Section 1	*Exploring New Country: The Expeditions*	12
	Custer, 1874	16
	Dodge-Newton-Jenney, 1875	24
	Crook, 1876	37
Section 2	*Seeking a Fortune: Gold in the Hills*	42

After the Custer Expedition's gold discovery (and the massive publicity surrounding that event), the rush was on. By the summer of 1875 there were hundreds of miners searching the Hills.

Section 3	*Building Towns & Cities*	120

The railroad reached Custer in 1890 and was completed all the way to Deadwood by the following year, signalling a new era in the Black Hills. Wagon trains, stagecoaches and other trappings of pioneer times began to disappear from daily use as the 20th Century dawned.

Section 4	*Seeing the Sights: The Beautiful Black Hills*	200

In the waning years of the 19th century, the Black Hills saw another change: a shift from people coming here only to seek their fortune, to those coming to see the sights and enjoy the natural beauty of the area.

Project Notes	294
Bibliography	299
Acknowledgments	300
Index	302

Preface

As part of America's move west, the Euro-American invasion of the Black Hills came late. While some fur trappers and explorers visited the region in the early 19th Century, the American incursion into the Hills really began with the Custer Expedition of 1874, which then sparked the Black Hills gold rush. By the time of the Black Hills rush, California had been a state for 25 years, and the rushes to Colorado and Montana had been over for more than decade. The nation was ready for another gold rush in 1874, and with the discovery of gold in the Hills excitement spread throughout the country.

Part of that excitement came because the Panic of 1873 had caused the nation to slip into an economic depression, and all Americans saw hope with the new gold discoveries. Some looked to the Black Hills as a way to regain their lost fortunes. Others, such as Midwestern farmers, thought they could find a fortune for the first time, while prospectors from Montana and Colorado looked at the Black Hills as another place to try their luck. And then many easterners who never planned to travel west hoped the new gold find would put the nation back onto the road to recovery. No matter their take, Americans had dreams and aspirations about this remote region known as the Black Hills, and all were curious about what might unfold.

Luckily for those who were curious, the timing was right to get news about the Hills. Telegraph lines stretched across the country, and newspaper correspondents followed the invaders into the Hills. But more to our concern, photography had become relatively commonplace by 1874, and images of the region immediately circulated eastward. William Illingworth shot photos of Custer's trip through the Hills in 1874, and in 1875 a relatively unknown photographer named Guerin shot the second set of images ever made here, during the Dodge-Newton-Jenney Expedition. Stanley J. Morrow followed General Crook and his men through the Hills in 1876, at the end of their so-called "Horsemeat March." Not only did photographers cover military expeditions, they also took pictures of the early diggings and the burgeoning boomtowns, and these impressions were new to America. While cameras existed during the time of the California rush, and were certainly available during the Colorado and Montana booms, few photographers ventured west to capture these early images. The Black Hills then offered an opportunity for Americans to take in scenes of a gold rush as it unfolded.

As the gold rush matured into a stable economic venture, photographers continued to come, and there was plenty to attract their attention. The Homestake gold mine rapidly developed into the most important mine in North America, and while the Homestake prospered, other mine owners in the northern Black Hills experimented with a number of ore processing techniques, such as smelting, chlorination and cyanide. These developments were of interest to many. By 1900 pundits labeled the area around Deadwood and Lead as the "richest ten square miles on earth," and with such fame came more photographers. In fact, much of the Black Hills enjoyed sustained economic growth after 1876, and this region, easily defined and relatively compact, continued to catch the nation's fancy. This interest became particularly apparent when Gutzon Borglum came to the Hills to carve a monument in the side of a mountain. By 1930 many thousands of photographs had been taken of the Black Hills, depicting about any and every scene imaginable, leaving a veritable treasure trove of what today are historical images.

While it is easy to lump all of these old photos together as historic, in reality different motivations lie behind many of them. Some photographers, such as Illingworth and Morrow, were professionals who hoped to sell their images to curious easterners. Many other commercial photographers followed them to the Hills, such as John C. H. Grabill who, in the late 1880s, set up a shop in Deadwood and soon had hundreds of images for sale. Some commercial photographers came to do promotional work for such entities as railroads and business clubs. Photographer J.E. Stimson took pictures in the Hills for the Union Pacific Railroad, while the Black Hills Mining Men's Association employed photographers to take hundreds of images of people, mines and towns that were used in the 1904 book *The Black Hills Illustrated*. This glossy, oversized publication was designed to attract more investors to the region. Of course, many other professional photographers established permanent studios in the Black Hills. And finally there were people like my grandmother, an amateur who owned an early box camera and recorded scenes as varied as the Needles

(Left) Detail, 1880s Rapid City Auditor's document.
(Facing page) "Bound for the Wind — the First Coach" from an 1877 Black Hills guidebook.
(Both Minnilusa Pioneer Museum)

or the railroad in Spearfish Canyon, just for fun. No matter the motivation of the photographers, the Black Hills has a well recorded past.

Having old pictures and understanding them, however, can be two different things. While we often look at old photos to rekindle memories of days long gone, it must be remembered that these images can be the basis of historical research. From these photographs come the basic questions of history: the who, why, what and where. Pictures of people, buildings or any other subject will spark such questions as: Who were these people? Why was that building built? What was going on there? Where was that taken? These types of questions are only the beginning of what photographs can do for historical inquiry, for they are some of the best primary source documents available. They allow us to travel through time to witness the environment, the fashions, the architecture, and those things that were important to past generations. Photos are our visual link to the past and, in the case of the Black Hills, our starting point for understanding the past.

We in the Black Hills are not only lucky to have an exciting history, and to have many photos that connect us to our past, but we are also lucky to have books like this one to help us interpret that history. Author Paul Horsted understands how historic photos help us touch the past. He understands that a photo is just a glimpse in time, and while that glimpse may spur the fundamental questions of history, in reality history is much more: it is a continuum; it is about change over time, and it is about how we got to today from where we started 125 years ago. Paul's rephotography project, as presented in this book, demonstrates that change over time and gives us that visual link to the past. To use a hackneyed expression, Paul's photo combinations "make history come alive," for they allow us to imagine a continuous parade of events at that spot where the photo pairs were taken.

In some ways, Paul's efforts at rephotography are not unique. A number of other rephotography books have been produced, but there are some fundamental differences. Some of the other rephotography books feature the work of just one photographer, as Paul and Ernest Grafe's *Exploring with Custer* does with Illingworth. In this new effort, however, Paul has sought out a variety of images that span the width and breadth of the Black Hills. Another difference is that some rephotography books have hidden messages. Sometimes they want to show how dramatically the natural environment has changed, and that kind of book is really a call for stronger protectionist policies. While environmental change will be evident in this book, that is certainly not Paul's point. Instead, Paul is first and foremost an artist. He wants to present the best images possible, reproduced to the most exacting standards. This book is a work of art. Secondary for Paul, but of primary importance to his readers, is the fact that he is a historian, and a good one. Paul researches his locations, picks pictures that offer the most complete sweep of Black Hills history, and, when in doubt, he asks others for help. Paul's historical inquiry is every bit as impeccable as his artistry, and those qualities are seldom seen in other rephotography projects.

With this book Paul has then conjoined artistry and history, but it has not been easy for him. I have had the pleasure of watching Paul work, and this must be the most ambitious project he has ever undertaken. With the Custer Expedition book, for instance, Paul had a finite number of Illingworth shots to select from, he had some idea where Custer had traveled, and many of the sites had been researched earlier. With this new venture, Paul had to cull through thousands of photographs at numerous archives and libraries, and then select those that offered the best story. Also, in some instances, Paul had only the vaguest of ideas where a photo might have been taken, and locating that exact spot took countless hours of scouting and experimentation. But Paul's determination and drive for perfection kept him motivated to check another library or climb another hill.

This beautiful book is truly a testament to Paul's talent and perseverance. Also, it shows his dedication to the artistry that is Black Hills history. Just like *Exploring with Custer*, this book will rapidly become a Black Hills classic. Some will proudly display it on their coffee tables, others will use it as a field guide, but most readers will enjoy it for its history and art. I just hope that 100 years from now another talented photographer will come along and add a third photo to each of Paul's sets. Then our descendants will be re-inspired by Black Hills history as they, too, touch the past through photographs, and they will realize all over again that history is about change over time.

David Wolff, Ph.D.
Spearfish, S.D., May 1, 2006

Introduction

The images in this book, old and new, are the result of a four-year project that grew almost of its own accord out of the earlier book *Exploring with Custer: The 1874 Black Hills Expedition*, which I co-authored with Ernest Grafe. In that volume, Ernie and I traced the route of Custer's wagon train through the Black Hills, mapped the Expedition's campsites, and quoted from diaries, journals and newspaper reports written by the men who explored the Black Hills in 1874. The idea was to bring this history alive for readers by making it easy to follow much of Custer's Trail while reading the first-hand accounts of exploration and discovery.

In the second half of the book, we also traced the movements of photographer William H. Illingworth, who accompanied the Expedition and took the very first photographs of the Black Hills. With help from earlier researchers, landowners and other sources, we found the locations where Illingworth had set up his camera and tripod. We then attempted to "rephotograph" the scenes precisely as he had composed them, to show the Black Hills of "then and now." If the photo site was on public land, we identified the location so readers could experience it first-hand.

The Custer Expedition project gave me a deep appreciation for the insights that historic photography could provide. When I stood at the very place where a picture had been made 125 years earlier and contemplated the changes and similarities before me, whether man-made or natural, I found it an ideal way to *connect* to the scene, and the history, contained within those hazy, sepia-toned photographs. Formerly mysterious images suddenly had a context, creating a link between past and present. This gave the historic photos a much deeper level of meaning. They became more real, almost like a photo I had taken myself and remembered well.

Finding each photo site was also deeply rewarding in itself. It meant solving a "history mystery," in a way, and I enjoyed it immensely. More than once, my heart beat a little faster when I realized I had reached the location of a Custer Expedition photo, when I first sighted that same rock or tree stump visible in the 1874 image. I would feel as if I might turn around and glimpse Mr. Illingworth moving off into the trees, or see the imprint of his tripod legs still visible on the ground before me.

Shortly after *Exploring with Custer* was published, I received a request to "rephotograph" an image made by another pioneering photographer, Stanley J. Morrow of Yankton, Dakota Territory, who had been in the Black Hills in 1876 and 1877. He had made dozens of stereoview images here, including some not far from my home near Custer. The location of the image requested was already known, and I once again found myself standing in the footsteps of one of my photographic predecessors. (See page 38. And thank you, Paul Hedren, for introducing me to Mr. Morrow's work.)

This venture got my mind (and my feet) moving more quickly along a path it had already started after the publication of *Exploring with Custer*. Using the work of several early photographers rather than just one, wouldn't it be interesting to find and rephotograph dozens or even hundreds of early historic photo sites across the region? One disappointment with photos from the 1874 Expedition was that Custer's route left large areas — such as Spearfish Canyon, Deadwood Gulch and the Badlands — unexplored and therefore undocumented. I was curious to see if changes seen at most of the 1874 photo sites — for example the tremendous tree growth — were also present in these other areas, and to learn whether there were other changes, or similarities, to be found.

I began visiting archives, museums, private photo collectors and the Internet, looking for historic images of the Black Hills. Initially I planned to rephotograph only samples from the earliest military expeditions (1874-76) as well as the earliest possible historic images of existing cities and landmarks. Then I began finding old photos of good-sized towns that once had "boomed" but had since faded into near-oblivion (Crook City and Cyanide are examples). These were too fascinating to pass by. Another discovery was the many wonderful images of Devil's Tower from as early as 1875, and of the Badlands from just a few years later. I began to expand my definition of the Black Hills "region" to the area more or less within view of the Hills, including towns like Newell, Belle Fourche, Wall and Sundance.

I also found fascinating shots taken after the pioneer era, post-1890 images of growing towns, working ranches, and the coming of the railroads. And I saw yet another interesting transition

(Left) Composing a "modern" photo above Sylvan Lake with the help of a reference print. (Paul Horsted photo)

(Facing page) Deadwood's Main Street, 1876. (Adams Museum & House/Photographer unknown)

involving people who came to the Black Hills not so much to find their fortune as to enjoy its scenic beauty. As railroads reached into the Hills in the early 1890s, a new personality type appeared in the photographic record: the tourist. In these images we see outings by train to the falls in Spearfish Canyon; people in rowboats in front of a grand lodge on Sylvan Lake; hardy climbers on top of Harney Peak; and, eventually, travelers gazing in wonder at granite faces emerging from a cliff above Keystone.

With this expanded scope, the images here comprise the work of approximately 50 different photographers — amateur, professional, and many who were unidentified. Some visited the Hills for only a week or two; others lived here for decades. I've taken some care to present their work almost as if you were looking at the original print in a museum or archive, complete with dog-eared corners, stains, fly-specks and the marks of previous owners. Digital tools have been applied to enhance image *clarity*, because I believe all details should be as clear as possible, but I resisted doing much "restoration" in cleaning up defects and dirt. I love the time-worn character of these images and have tried to leave that character intact. I took some obvious digital liberties with stereoview images, replacing one pane with my matching modern image (always leaving the clearest of the two panes, whether left or right). I have liked this technique of combining "then and now" since first trying it with images of the Custer Expedition.

The caption associated with each photo pair provides a brief introduction to the activity or scene, both past and present. One of the difficult aspects of this project was trying to find accurate information about the historic photos and their content. Very few of the original images carry caption information, and most are not dated (thus the use of "circa 1890" or similar descriptions). Many prints do not even carry the name of the photographer. The information provided is the best I could find in the many excellent local and regional histories available, and in talking with local historical authorities (noted in the Acknowledgments, page 300). These sources helped me fill the many gaps in my own knowledge of Black Hills history. My ultimate goal, however, was not to write the story of every locality (another book in itself!) but rather to present what I found at each camera site along with an overview of that area's history. If you find your interest piqued by a certain place, I hope you will consult the fine books in the bibliography for more information. And if you think I've missed something important, please let me know.

A *Field Note* accompanies many captions. These are personal notations I made as I visited and rephotographed each site and I hope readers will find them useful. For those who are interested in even greater detail, please consult the *Project Notes* beginning on page 294. Here you will find more information about the project, including how the photo sites were found and rephotographed; some conclusions about what we can learn from the images; technical data; and more.

Adjacent to the modern image in each photo pair you will find the date it was taken, for reference and posterity. GPS data is also provided for the many photos taken on public land, for those readers who wish to visit the sites and experience the historical treasure that some provide.

I enjoyed this project more than almost anything I've done in 25 years as a photographer in South Dakota — the past 10 in the Black Hills — and I hope this book won't be the end of it. I'm sure there are many historic Black Hills photos still awaiting rediscovery in attics and archives. I feel as if I've just scratched the surface of what could be done with the many thousands of historic photographs taken in the Black Hills, and I am cautiously optimistic that someday there will be a second volume or an expansion of *The Black Hills Yesterday & Today*. There is certainly enough history here to warrant it.

This book proved to be a great opportunity to get to know the Black Hills in an entirely new way, and I hope you will be able to see this area in a new way as well. After hiking hilltops from Hot Springs and Edgemont up to Spearfish and Belle Fourche, from the Badlands over to Devil's Tower, and from Rapid City to Sundance — as well as all the other interesting places where pioneer photographers placed their cameras — I find I'm getting a good idea of the geography not only of the present, but also of the past. I can hardly drive through the Hills now without envisioning the sepia scenes recorded by the early photographers. These visions are never far from my mind as the Black Hills continue to be developed, and, for better or worse, as they move further from their storied, historic past into the future.

I've selected a wide range of subject matter and locations to represent the amazing changes — and surprising similarities — found across the region. As you browse the following pages, I hope you enjoy stepping back in time and that you'll share with me the feeling of "standing in history" as you ponder these scenes of our beautiful *Black Hills Yesterday & Today*.

Paul Horsted
Custer, S.D., June 1, 2006

Key to the Photographs

This lists the collection in which the historic photograph was found and the photographer's name if known.

ADAMS MUSEUM & HOUSE/POLLOCK & BOYDEN

7-10-04 • N 43 54 19.1 W 103 32 09.1 • SOUTHEAST

Listed here are the date of the original photo (or "circa" if the date is unknown) as well as its title in "quotes." If a title does not appear on the original image, a descriptive name is supplied by the author.

This data includes the date the new photo was taken, followed by a GPS reading at the location (except on private property or in unusual circumstances) and the direction the camera was facing. If the GPS reading also says "vicinity," it is for a nearby public location where the site may be observed. (Map datum WGS 84 was used here.)

Circa 1885

Palmer Gulch & Elkhorn Mountain

There is no data on the back of this stereoview except the imprint of photographer Pollock & Boyden. It appears to be one of a series they took around the north and west sides of the Harney Peak range. None of the men are identified, unfortunately, nor is the purpose of that notebook one of them is holding.

The modern site was found, after several days of searching, in the heart of Palmer Gulch, which is now home to tourist lodges and a campground resort. One side of the valley is lined by a long ridge of broken rocks like the ones seen here, requiring a great deal of study before the matching view could be located. A fallen tree leans across the gap in the modern image.

Field notes are occasionally listed at the bottom of the page, providing descriptions of what the author encountered at the site or other observations.

Field Note: I have usually resisted re-creating elements seen in the historic photos, but in this case I felt a stand-in for the pioneering photographer's assistants was needed. With a self-timer on my tripod-mounted camera, I walked into the scene holding another camera as well as a copy of the original historic photo.

Exploring New Country

The earliest images of the Black Hills were recorded on glass plates in the cameras of intrepid photographers who joined military and civilian expeditions venturing into this relatively uncharted territory. These first pictures of the landscape, dim and soft, are a window on how the Black Hills looked before there were roads, mines, towns or cities.

Images from these three Expeditions — led by Custer, Dodge and Crook — show us the beginnings of the gold rush and some of its consequences. The photographs also pave the way historically for the camera-toting men and women who would follow miners and settlers to the Black Hills.

The 1874 Black Hills "Custer" Expedition

The first photographs of the Black Hills were made in the summer of 1874 by William Henry Illingworth, a St. Paul photographer who accompanied Gen. George Armstrong Custer's exploring party of a thousand soldiers and civilians. Illingworth, a master of his craft, made photographs at several campsites across the Black Hills, including a well-known image of the General with a grizzly bear he shot near present-day Rochford. The Illingworth photographs on the following pages (with comparative images taken in 2004 and 2005) are selected from the book *Exploring With Custer: The 1874 Black Hills Expedition*, by Ernest Grafe and Paul Horsted (www.custertrail.com).

Custer and his troops were in the Black Hills for about three weeks, during which gold was found on French Creek by civilian miners who had accompanied the Expedition. The well-publicized discovery would spark increasing conflict with the Lakota Sioux — who had been guaranteed ownership of the Black Hills under the Fort Laramie Treaty of 1868 — and lead to further Federal and military action in the field.

The 1875 Dodge-Newton-Jenney Expedition

News of gold brought a rush of fortune-hunters eager to cash in on "the new El Dorado." The government tried at first to keep these intruders out, while sending another expedition to conduct a more thorough survey of the Hills in the summer of 1875. The objective was to verify reports of gold and to place a value on the region that could be used in purchase negotiations with the Lakota Sioux. Col. Richard Irving Dodge led the expedition, commanding a military escort for civilian geologists Henry Newton and Walter P. Jenney.

Much less is known about Fritz Guerin, a photographer who joined this expedition. His Black Hills images seem to be published only on stereoview mounts carrying the name of a St. Louis photographer, Robert Benecke. It would appear that Guerin sold his Black Hills negatives to Benecke, who then published the images under his own label — a common practice among photographers at the time. Guerin's images are not as well done, either in composition or technical quality, as those made by Illingworth in 1874. But the images included here offer tantalizing additional glimpses of the Black Hills in a near-virgin state, still without formally established towns.

The 1876 Crook Expedition (Starvation March)

By late 1875, the U.S. Government had abandoned the idea of purchasing the Black Hills from the Lakota Sioux and ceased its efforts to keep whites out of the area. Growing anger among the Sioux, along with pressure from the Army, led to Custer's defeat at the Little Big Horn in June of 1876 — and to a fascinating but much less known march led by Gen. George Crook in the fall of that year.

Searching for Indians thought to have participated in the Custer debacle, Crook and his troops found a band of Sioux at the Slim Buttes (about 80 miles north of the Black Hills) on Sept. 9. After an intense battle that saw casualties on both sides, Crook captured a few Indians who indeed had in their possession items taken from U.S. soldiers at the Little Big Horn. Soldiers and captives then began marching to the Black Hills.

Crook's troops had been poorly supplied and were already going hungry before the battle. There was little or no grass for the horses and mules along the way, and soon the men and their mounts were starving. By the time the troops reached a campsite near present-day Whitewood (on Sept. 13), the soldiers had begun eating horses and mules as they collapsed from exhaustion and lack of fodder along the trail.

Relief wagons came out from Crook City and saved the starving soldiers, and eventually they recuperated in camps near the present-day towns of Custer and Pringle. Several photographers were already working in the Hills in the fall of 1876, and at least one — Stanley J. Morrow of Yankton, Dakota Territory — recorded a number of images of Crook's soldiers. A selection of these images by Morrow, another outstanding pioneer photographer, is presented here.

"Wagon Train Passing Through Castle Creek Valley"
8-23-05 • N 44 04 25.1 W 103 54 24.8 • Northwest

(Facing page) A stereoview by W.H. Illingworth (inset) shows more than 100 wagons of the Black Hills Expedition in Castle Creek Valley on July 26, 1874. In the modern color image made at this location, the same limestone formations and, remarkably, several burned stumps seen in the 1874 image are still present today. (Paul Horsted Collection/Illingworth)

Field Note: The connection to the past is almost tangible when you gaze upon those rock formations and surviving tree stumps. If you go, please add nothing to or take anything from this scene.

(Left) Image by Stanley J. Morrow of the Crook Expedition, 1876. (W.H. Over Museum/Morrow)

Exploring New Country: The Expeditions

8-3-05 • N 44 01 42.2 W 103 50 41.7 • NORTH

Custer Expedition: July 26, 1874
"Lime Stone Peak and Castle Creek Valley"

Custer's wagon train is just rolling into camp in this image made in the valley a mile above present-day Deerfield Lake. Lime Stone Peak is now a tree-covered mountain rising above the historic campsite.

Field Note: I originally rephotographed this scene — and the other 1874 images in this section — in the year 2000. If you have a copy of *Exploring With Custer*, compare the images there with those shown here, all taken in 2005. The growth of small trees is clearly visible over the five-year span. In 2000 there were no trees in the foreground of this image, while today at least a dozen small pines have taken root. In another ten years (barring a thinning program or fire) this site on U.S. Forest Service property will be blocked by trees.

Sioux Camp in Castle Creek Valley.

8-3-05 • N 44 02 02.2 W 103 50 42.3 • SOUTHEAST

Custer Expedition July 26-27, 1874
"Sioux Camp in Castle Creek Valley"

In another view of the campsite on the opposite page, Illingworth captured a high scenic view of the Castle Creek Valley with rows of tents and circled wagons visible in the middle distance. Part of the horse herd grazes at left. The title refers to remnants of an Indian camp site found here, recently deserted by a band of Lakota Sioux who were encountered several miles up the valley.

The modern image shows a gravel road that now runs down the valley toward the small town of Deerfield, which is just barely visible in the distance.

Field Note: A modest hike from the road brings you to this beautiful though partially tree-blocked view of the former camp site. Cool your feet in Castle Creek upon your return to the valley below.

Custer Expedition Aug. 1-5, 1874
Permanent Camp on French Creek

One of the few panoramic images Illingworth made during the Black Hills Expedition, this is possibly his most stunning view. Smoke rises into the air above dozens of tents, wagons and grazing horses and mules. The soldiers camped here from Aug. 1 to Aug. 5, 1874, while reconnaissance parties explored the country to the south and east. One party passed through what is now known as Custer State Park while another party, under Gen. Custer, reached the Cheyenne River near present-day Edgemont.

It was from this camp that news of a gold strike was sent to the outside world.

4-28-06 • N 43 46 24.0 W 103 32 16.0 • SOUTHWEST

About three miles east of Custer, modern campgrounds and a cabin or two now occupy the site where the town's namesake spent part of a week during the summer of 1874. Gold discoveries on French Creek, which winds through the middle of the photograph, contributed to the hostilities that would erupt at Little Big Horn two years later.

Field Note: This site is on U.S. Forest Service property and easily approached from America Center Road.

Custer Expedition: Aug. 1-5, 1874
Permanent Camp and Harney Peak Range

Illingworth made a second panoramic image of the Aug. 1-5 camp site from a vantage point above French Creek. Harney Peak and the Needles are just visible in the far distance, while part of present-day Calamity Peak is seen at upper left, framing the tents and wagons below.

This was the southernmost point reached by the Expedition as a whole. After camping and exploring here for five days, Custer and his 1,000 men began their return trek, winding through the Black Hills and finally emerging near Bear Butte on Aug. 16.

8-12-05 • N 43 45 58.0 W 103 32 18.3 • NORTH

Today, Highway 16A crosses through the heart of Custer's 1874 camp, where a commercial campground now offers a less rustic though still scenic experience in this historic valley. Military expeditions of 1875 and 1876 also used the area as a campsite (see following pages), adding lesser-known chapters to the lore of the Black Hills.

Field Note: This photo site, a high rock prominent above the valley, is where Illingworth made several other views of this camp and vicinity, all shown in the book *Exploring With Custer*. It is a beautiful place to have a picnic lunch and ponder the changes that have taken place in more than 100 years of Black Hills history.

Exploring New Country: The Expeditions

Gold Mountain Range and Headquarters.

8-12-05 • N 43 45 58.0 W 103 32 18.3 • Northwest

Custer Expedition: Aug. 1-5, 1874
"Gold Mountain Range and Headquarters"

Illingworth's view at left shows a corner of the Aug. 1-5 Expedition camp site, including Custer's tent, which under close examination is different than the other tents in camp (see opposite page for a clearer view).

The "Gold Mountain Range" is now known by several names. The west end of Calamity Peak is visible at upper right, as is part of the Buckhorn Range behind it. The outline of Crazy Horse Memorial is almost lost in the distant shadows of the modern view.

Custer Expedition: Aug. 7, 1874
"Our First Grizzly, Killed by General Custer"

Diary and newspaper accounts left by those who were with Custer in 1874 make it clear that he was not the only one shooting at "his" grizzly. The other men posing with their guns contributed to its demise. From left, they are Bloody Knife, a Ree Indian and Custer's Chief of Scouts; Custer; Pvt. Noonan, Custer's orderly; and Capt. William Ludlow, Chief Engineer of the Expedition.

At right, the rocks where the grizzly lay look surprisingly different in color, covered with lichen and seemingly darker than they appear to be in the historic image.

Exploring New Country: The Expeditions

4-28-06 • Private Land • Northwest

1875 Dodge-Newton-Jenney Expedition
"Indians & Interpreters" and "Indian Chieves & Interpreters"

In the two historic images shown here, white men pose with Indians in an apparently cordial setting. On the opposite page, one native holds an American flag while others wear hats that were typical of gift items from whites in that era. The diary of Col. Richard Irving Dodge, military commander of the 1875 Black Hills Expedition, twice mentions groups of Indians visiting camp in the company of whites. One group was made up of representatives of the Indian agencies from which the Federal Government was hoping to negotiate the purchase of the Black Hills.

In the modern photograph, Calamity Peak still forms a backdrop to the valley where Dodge was encamped. America Center Road cuts through the center of the image, which was taken on private property.

Field Note: By looking carefully at the arrangement of rock outcroppings on Calamity Peak, I was able to find the location that seems to be exactly where this group posed in 1875.

1875 Dodge-Newton-Jenney Expedition
"Miners at Work on French Creek"

Following Custer's 1874 discovery of gold in the Black Hills, miners quickly rushed to the region in search of fortune. This group is already digging to bedrock along French Creek in early 1875, just half a mile west of present-day downtown Custer. Note the tripod of rifles at the ready, and the sluice box that is washing gravel dug from the pit.

In the modern image, the same rocks are glimpsed through trees in the background. This is presently a vacant area between hotels, with a "for sale" sign in front of it as this book went to press.

The photographer for the 1875 Black Hills Expedition was named Guerin, but — in contrast to Illingworth the year before — very little is known about him. He may have sold his negatives after returning to civilization, for the only known images from 1875 are printed on card stock bearing the name of Robert Benecke of St. Louis.

Field Note: I was lucky indeed to spot the rock formations in the background as I drove through Custer one day. In retrospect, the location of this image "makes sense," since the photographer likely passed by en route to the known 1875 campsite three miles east of present-day Custer.

4-28-06 • N 43 46 12.4 W 103 31 47.9 • SOUTHWEST

1875 Dodge-Newton-Jenney Expedition
"Stockade on French Creek"

The structure in the original image was built by a small party of miners, led by a man named Gordon, who followed Custer's Trail into the Black Hills and reached French Creek in December 1874. The men posing in the foreground are not identified; the nearest appears to be dressed in Native American style.

The "Gordon Stockade" in the modern image is the third replica built on the site and appears to be in precisely the same location as the original.

The historic site is just inside the border of Custer State Park. Interpretive programs are presented here during the summer months.

Exploring New Country: The Expeditions

8/20/05 • N 43 50 57.5 W 103 32 18.8 • EAST

1875 Dodge-Newton-Jenney Expedition
"Saw Teeth Near Harney Peak"

The "saw teeth" (now known as the Cathedral Spires) are seen here from a location in present-day Custer State Park, not far off Trail 4 in the wilderness system around Harney Peak. Although there would have been no established trails when this image was made in 1875, it is reasonable to assume that the photographer set up his camera here while traveling to or from Harney Peak, where other photos were taken.

The site today is overgrown with trees, but the foreground rocks firmly establish the original location.

Field Note: It was very satisfying to at last locate this site, now deeply buried in woods. I saw the background (see a more recent view on page 254) and eventually located the foreground rocks, which are nearly covered in vegetation.

8-22-05 • N 43 51 54.4 W 103 31 52.5 • NORTH

1875 Dodge-Newton-Jenney Expedition
"Harney's Pass on Harney's Peak"

"Harney's Pass" is a gap in the mass of granite that forms the summit of this famous mountain. The wall at right is part of the pinnacle in the photograph on page 33, which surveyors have climbed to work on a new map.

Unfortunately, early photographic plates did not penetrate haze very well, as seen (or not seen) here, so distant objects are obscured. But it is interesting to note the spruce tree at right in the historic photo; its skeleton survives in the modern image, as another apparently does at center.

Facing Page: 8-22-05 • N 43 51 50.9 W 103 31 53.7 • South

1875 Dodge-Newton-Jenney Expedition
"Saw-Teeth Near Harney's Peak."

The "Saw Teeth" were called "Pipe Organs" the year before by Custer and his men. Today they are known as the Cathedral Spires, while the large granite mass at right is now called Little Devil's Tower because of its resemblance to the well-known Wyoming landmark (also photographed in 1875; see page 35).

The modern view of this area is remarkably unchanged, although some of the live trees in the foreground of the historic image remain only as dead wood today. A denser forest obscures some rock formations visible in the 1875 photo, and brown areas indicate areas of pine infested with insects that have killed these trees.

Exploring New Country: The Expeditions

8-22-05 • N 43 51 54.3 W 103 31 49.0 • NORTHEAST

1875 Dodge-Newton-Jenney Expedition
"View from Summit of Harney's Peak"

Despite his title, the photographer hadn't quite reached the summit of Harney for this photograph. But he was very close. The historic image was taken from the southeast (right) side of the pinnacle shown on the opposite page. It is a view toward the northeast, with part of present-day Elkhorn Mountain visible at far right. Note once again the inability of early photographic emulsions to penetrate haze and capture the valleys in the distance.

8-22-05 • N 43 51 55.3 W 103 31 51.8 • Northeast

1875 Dodge-Newton-Jenney Expedition
"Surveying Party on the Summit of Harney's Peak"

This may be a view of the first ascent of Harney Peak. Three men (one seated at left) are preparing a surveyor's transit, presumably working on a more detailed map of the Black Hills. Gen. Custer had reached the base of this pinnacle a year earlier, but, lacking rope and ladders, he and his men were unable to make the final ascent in the short time they were here.

This "summit" is about 200 feet south of the summit where hikers now climb to the stone fire tower. The other peak may have been too difficult to ascend in 1875 for the purpose of surveying, or the explorers may have believed that this pinnacle was higher.

The man at upper right appears to be the expedition's topographer, Valentine McGillycuddy, who is generally credited with being the first to climb Harney Peak. After his death in 1939, his ashes were interred in the base of the stone fire tower nearby.

Field Note: I'm not sure, but the two large trees in the foreground of the new photo may be the same two seen at near left in the historic photo. Certainly the same two or three oval rocks lie behind them. It is very difficult to accurately rephotograph an image when the background is obscured.

Exploring New Country: The Expeditions

Above: 10-12-05 • Private Land • South   Facing Page: 9-28-05 • N 44 35 23.2 W 104 42 06.4 • West

1875 Dodge-Newton-Jenney Expedition
"Inyan Kara & Camp Bradley"; "Bear Lodge from East"

Col. Dodge camped here twice (above), Aug. 25-29 and again on Sept. 9, and this image was made on one of these occasions. Inyan Kara is a well-known landmark on the west side of the Black Hills, near the place where Custer found an entrance the year before. The camp location is now private land.

The first images ever made of "Bear Lodge" (facing page) were taken during the 1875 Expedition. Chief geologist Jenney's map used the Native American name for the monolith, but the map made under Col. Dodge labelled it "Devil's Tower," which is now the commonly used name.

Field Note, Facing page: I prefer "Bear Lodge," the traditional Native American name for this stunning work of nature. The photo site is just a few yards north of the main road into Devil's Tower National Monument.

Exploring New Country: The Expeditions

8-8-05 • Private Land • East

1875 Dodge-Newton-Jenney Expedition
"Camp Harney on French Creek"

Tents belonging to the 1875 Black Hills Expedition fill the valley on the site of Custer's "Permanent Camp" of the year before, although this camp stretches further down the valley. The Gordon Stockade is visible as a brown line at center left. The man standing in the foreground appears to be physician Valentine T. McGillycuddy, the expedition's surveyor, who is seen in other photographs of that year. In later years he would become a respected Indian agent and attend to the dying Crazy Horse.

The modern view, taken from private property, shows the well-preserved pasture and a graceful home that now lie where so much history has taken place.

4-28-06 • N 43 46 11.5 W 103 31 46.4 • West

1876 Crook Expedition
"Troops Passing Old Stockade"

The Gordon Stockade was less than two years "old" when Morrow recorded this view of Crook's men posing in formation. Crook himself is seated on a horse at right.

Note that the foreground ditch is now filled with reeds. The creation of nearby Stockade Lake raised the water table, at times filling this drainage with water and causing a change in vegetation.

The present-day Gordon Stockade was rebuilt in 2005, and looks nearly identical to the original. The Custer Lutheran Fellowship church can be seen at far right, across Highway 16A which now passes nearby.

Gordon Stockade is just inside the west boundary of Custer State Park.

8-27-03 • PRIVATE LAND • NORTHEAST

1876 Crook Expedition
"Gen. Crook's Army in Camp, on French Creek, Below Old Stockade"

This camp is one of home-made shelters and disorder as veterans of Gen. Crook's recent "Starvation March" continue to recuperate east of present-day Custer. The title may be in error; another title, "Army Camp (in Wickups) on French Creek," seems to better fit this site which is above (upstream from) the stockade, not below it (see next spread for the camp site "below.") "Wick-ups" is a term for the crude shelters made of branches and blankets or canvas as seen above. This view is among the least changed from past to present in this book. Foreground rocks remain undisturbed, as do larger formations such as Calamity Peak in the distance. A private road now cuts across the hill in the middle ground.

Field Note: My thanks to Paul Hedren for telling me exactly where to find this location and for loaning me the original stereoview shown here.

5-16-06 • N 43 45 11.5 W 103 38 04.7 • NORTHEAST

1876 Crook Expedition
"Supply Train in Corral, Near Custer City"

Gen. Crook's troops received desperately needed relief when a wagon train loaded with supplies arrived near Custer in the fall of 1876. It is not clear what is going on in this image, because most of the soldiers have stopped what they were doing to pose for the camera. The front axle of one wagon appears to be removed, perhaps for repair. A "corral" or two made of saddles can be glimpsed in the background.

The modern image was taken just west of Custer, looking across private property to Highway 16, which now cuts through the site. (Note cars passing by on an artificially elevated roadbed.)

Field Note: You can view this site from the parking lot of Black Hills Electric Cooperative west of Custer.

Exploring New Country: The Expeditions

8-12-05 • N 43 46 08.7 W 103 31 12.7 • SOUTHEAST

1876 Crook Expedition
"Gen. Crook's Army in Camp, on French Creek, Below Old Stockade"

Now supplied with tents and other equipment, Crook's troops regroup at another location along French Creek, about half a mile below the present-day Gordon Stockade. The foreground tent may well have belonged to miners working claims along this stretch of creek.

The modern-day view reveals a remarkable change: Stockade Lake has filled the valley following construction of a dam in the 1930s. The large rock at left remains in place, however, allowing us to confirm the exact site of the historic photo.

Field Note: Locating this site was one of the most delightful surprises of this entire project. I had noticed the background hills while looking out a church window (during a hymn, Pastor Dave, not the sermon!) at nearby Custer Lutheran Fellowship. I walked down French Creek the next day until I came to the foreground rock. There is a fairly obvious flat spot at this location, where I believe Morrow probably placed his tripod in 1876.

The Black Hills Yesterday & Today

5-08-06 • PRIVATE LAND • EAST

1876 Crook Expedition
"Gen. Crook's Army in Camp at Point of Rocks, Near Buffalo Gap, Black H."

Buffalo Gap may have been the nearest reference point when this image was made, but today the site is within view of the southern Black Hills town of Pringle. Some of Crook's tents and wagons are sheltered by the granite formations that gave this area its name in 1876, while the rest of the camp continues further up the valley.

In the modern image, it is remarkable to see how little change there has been in the shape of the creek bed.

Field Note: See page 297 for the image at the actual site of this photo, now blocked by tree branches. I moved about six feet south (right) to get the relatively clear view shown here, which is why the alignment of the creek bank with background elements is not as perfect as it could be.

41

Seeking A Fortune

After the Custer Expedition's gold discovery (and the massive publicity surrounding that event), the rush was on. The Gordon Party followed Custer's wagon trail into the Black Hills, arriving at French Creek and building a protective stockade there in December 1874. Other parties of gold-seekers also found their way into the Hills, and by the summer of 1875 there were at least several hundred miners scouring the area.

But it was quickly apparent that there were not vast quantities of gold waiting for them on French Creek. Knowledgeable miners (or those who found that all the claims had been taken) began to look elsewhere. Moving along Spring Creek, they established Hill City, Sheridan and other transitory mining camps. Camp Crook (later Pactola) was established about this time along Rapid Creek. Gold was found in all of these areas, yet the big strike was still to come.

A small party coming into the northern Hills from Montana in the fall of 1875 found gold in Deadwood Gulch, and the news spread quickly. Boom camps were soon "busted" as the action moved north to richer diggings. The towns of Custer and Hill City were virtually abandoned overnight (see pages 80-81). Then, on April 9, 1876, Moses and Fred Manuel explored a hillside with their partner, Hank Harney. On a branch of Gold Run Creek, high above what is now the Open Cut, they found some promising quartz that would prove to be their "home stake" — the strike that allowed them to go back home with plenty of money. The big "lead" they had found was destined to become the great Homestake Mine, which would shape the fortunes of the towns of Lead and Deadwood and the Black Hills for the next 130 years.

Several photographers were already working in the Black Hills by the summer of 1876, and their published work reflects this geographic change in focus. There are relatively few images of Custer City that are dated 1876, but many views of Deadwood and surrounding gulches taken during that year still survive. Deadwood and the northern Hills were where the action was, both in mining and in photography.

On the heels of the prospectors (and sometimes ahead of them) came the merchants, sawmill operators and saloon girls, along with all the amenities of civilization captured in the following images. The U.S. military, meanwhile, was under pressure to protect civilians traveling to and settling in the area. Having failed in its negotiations to purchase the Black Hills, and following the defeat of Custer and his men at the Little Big Horn in June 1876, the government began seeking a site for a military post near the gold camps. Troops set up a temporary camp in the shadow of Bear Butte during the summer of that year, and by 1878 Ft. Meade had been established a few miles away, on the northeast shoulder of the Hills.

A number of other towns and future cities had already sprung into being by then. Sturgis gained importance with its proximity to the new fort. Rapid City had been laid out in 1876, as were Spearfish and Crook City.

Hot Springs, though inhabited earlier, acquired its current name in 1883. Lesser-known towns such as Cyanide and Cambria would arrive later as well — and many of them would not survive. Keystone represents a kind of transition from one age to the next. It came into being with a new gold discovery in 1891, but would find its prosperity in tourism as the gateway to Mt. Rushmore in the 20th Century.

Most of the Black Hills continued to grow and prosper through the 1890s, as the rough-and-tumble times of the gold rush evolved into bustling towns and cities. When the railroad finally reached in from the plains, crossing the backbone of the Hills to connect the former mining camps of Custer and Deadwood by 1891, the pioneer era of the Black Hills was drawing to a close, just 17 years after Custer's wagons rolled in.

"Deadwood Looking North 1876"
5-3-06 • N 44 22 34.2 W 103 43 51.7 • *Northeast*

(Facing page) Stanley J. Morrow recorded this view of muddy Main Street in Deadwood at the height of the gold rush. The town had been thrown together in a short time, and all the buildings seen here had been constructed during the preceding few months — or were still under construction (right). The man standing with a transit at center left is not identified, but surveyors would certainly have been busy about this time, recording the many claims up and down Whitewood and Deadwood Creeks. (W.H. Over Museum)

(Facing page, inset) The modern view is taken from approximately the same location, looking north from upper Main Street. Much has changed here, with numerous brick buildings today replacing wooden ones (most of which burned in the catastrophic 1879 fire), and neat paving bricks eventually covering the mud-caked streets.

"A Trip to the Black Hills: Scene in Custer City."
(Below) Image from an article in **Scribner's Monthly** *written by Leander P. Richardson, April 1877. (Robert A. Farrar Collection)*

June 15, 1876
"Main Street, Deadwood"

This is certainly one of the earliest photographs — if not the first — of Deadwood's developing Main Street. Other 1876 images from about this angle show the same buildings in later stages of construction, and some of the trees seen here are missing in photos taken later that summer. Whitewood Creek is just off camera to the right.

The Black Hills Yesterday & Today

6-22-05 • N 44 22 34.3 W 103 43 52.4 • Northeast

Aside from the shape of distant hills, modern Deadwood bears little resemblance to its 1876 counterpart. Main Street appears to be in about the same position, although there is debate over whether it was moved slightly over time. Any surviving remnants of the 1876 scene are likely to be underground, beneath the more modern buildings, where they are occasionally unearthed by archaeologists working the sites of new construction.

Field Note: I believe the original image was taken from a small hill visible in other early photos of Deadwood, later excavated into the basement of the present-day Franklin Hotel. The nearest matching site I could find was from the balcony of the Franklin, overlooking Main Street.

47

Seeking a Fortune: Gold in the Hills

9-14-05 · PRIVATE LAND · SOUTH

Circa 1877
"Deadwood from McGovern Hill"

Photographer Stanley J. Morrow visited Deadwood in 1876. But it appears he was also here in 1877 and perhaps again in 1878 based on the titles of his published photographs. The amount of finished construction in this image suggests that it was taken during one of the later visits. The camera site (actually on present-day Forest Hill) was used by numerous photographers over the years to record the growth and change of Deadwood.

Field Note: A ridge of limestone runs for a hundred feet or so along this hilltop above town, providing many places for an early photographer's tripod to rest securely. I selected a vantage point that seemed to closely match Morrow's and that was not completely blocked by trees.

1876
"City of Deadwood, From North"

The earliest views of Deadwood can be identified by the pair of tall pines still standing on Main Street, a remnant of the forest that had filled the gulch just a few months earlier. The trees seen here have disappeared in later Main Street views. This image was made from a hillside on the lower end of Main, which has since been cut back to create a level area for additional buildings.

Deadwood today is also a place of new construction, as casinos and hotels (like the one at left) are built or upgraded as the town prospers under legalized gambling.

Field Note: The closest match I could find for this view was from the roof of Berg Jewelry, where the owners kindly let me spend an hour watching the passing scene below. It is hard to be certain, but the alignment of Main Street with the background hills points to this vicinity as being close to the original photo site. The GPS reading is for the public street level, not the roof.

Seeking a Fortune: Gold in the Hills

7-12-04 • N 44 23 08.5 W 103 43 08.0 • SOUTHWEST

Circa 1889
"Tollgate below Deadwood, S.D."

The title of this stereoview implies it was taken after South Dakota's 1889 statehood. Under magnification, the words on the side of the wagon read "The Specialty Photograph Co. Omaha," but no information about the photographer or the company is listed on the original stereoview. A sign on the adjacent building contains the words "gold dust" and what may be "25 cents," which was the toll for using a privately-built road between Deadwood and Centennial Prairie near Spearfish. Brown Rocks rises above the Tollgate and the present-day hotel/casino.

Field Note: Change is ever-present in the Black Hills. Since the modern image was made in 2004, the apartment building immediately behind the trolley was razed for an expansion of the nearby hotel/casino.

3-31-04 • Private Land • North

1883
"General View — Deadwood Flood"

Deadwood's history has been punctuated by disasters, including the 1883 flood that wiped out many buildings in its path. Whitewood Creek has now been routed beneath Highway 14A through much of the town.

The modern view is a near-approximation of the scene, complicated by the many changes that have occurred in the foreground.

The Black Hills Yesterday & Today

9-14-05 • PRIVATE LAND • SOUTH

1888
"Deadwood, Dakota"

On the facing page is an 1888 view of Deadwood from Forest Hill taken by photographer J.C.H. Grabill, a prolific commercial photographer who recorded hundreds of images of Black Hills towns, mines and landscapes.

Several brick buildings survive in the modern view, but the forest on the distant hills was burned off in the Grizzly Gulch fire of 2002.

Seeking a Fortune: Gold in the Hills

Circa 1895
Pluma

Pluma Junction linked the Burlington & Missouri River Railroad, which ran the length of the Black Hills (coming in from the upper left), with the Deadwood Central Railroad running up Gold Run Gulch (upper right) to Lead. Flooding seems to have been a problem here, though the rail bed escaped damage or has already been repaired.

The Black Hills Yesterday & Today

8-9-04 • Private land • Southwest

The roadbed of the former rail line is still visible in the modern scene. It is now the Mickelson Trail, also extending the length of the Black Hills. Pluma is still a junction, between Highways 85 (foreground) and 385. Visible on top of the mountain at right is the Yates Hoist Building of the Homestake Mining Company at nearby Lead.

Field Note: Clinging to what amounts to a cliff behind Twin City Hardware, I studied this scene for a while with the historic photo in hand. There may once have been a more solid camera position here, which has since fallen or eroded from the hillside.

Circa 1890
Deadwood Stage

This coach, en route to Deadwood from Spearfish, paused long enough for the unknown photographer to snap a photo about one mile north of town. A contingent of well-armed guards prominently display their weapons, and the man closest to the camera, sprawled on top of the stage, has only hooks for hands. (We can only wish for complete captions on these photos of 100 years ago!) Various stage routes operated in the Black Hills from 1876 until 1913, when the last stage ran on this route from Spearfish to Deadwood.

The Black Hills Yesterday & Today

6-22-05 • PRIVATE LAND • SOUTHEAST

The foreground here has gone through immense change since the original photo was taken. The narrow stage road has been widened over the years by cutting down several hundred yards of hillside, finally achieving the proportions of a four-lane highway (85) as Deadwood has grown.

The cliff in the middle distance is still in place (center left), although it too has changed through the effects of natural erosion, rockfalls and home construction. A new addition is Highway 14A in the distance, connecting Deadwood and Sturgis through Boulder Canyon.

Field Note: The original camera point is out in space, I believe, approximately 30 feet above the red car. I leaned out over the cliff as far as I could, and I shot this scene on two subsequent occasions trying to do better.

Seeking a Fortune: Gold in the Hills

7-14-04 • N 44 22 38.4 W 103 43 12.4 • NORTH

Circa 1876

"From White-Rock Looking down Whitewood"

The area around this site is still popularly known as "White Rocks." Only the title is written on the back of this particular stereoview, with no date or photographer, but another print of the scene is credited to Stanley J. Morrow. He probably shot the image in 1876, showing the lower (north) end of Deadwood. A 1959 fire cleared much of the forest from the hills in the distance.

Field Note: The top of the foreground cliff consists of crumbling, unstable limestone typical of the area above Deadwood known as White Rocks. However, I found that the original photographer was able to stand in relative safety behind the cliff top on a natural shelf, with a chest-high rock base conveniently in front of him, perfect both then and now for stabilizing a tripod.

8-5-04 • N 44 22 38.4 W 103 43 11.5 • Northeast

1876
"Anvill Rock from above Deadwood"

"Anvill" Rock is the formation at right in the historic photo. Made of the same crumbling limestone that gives White Rocks their name, the anvil itself has tumbled from the summit in the modern view.

The historic image provides an interesting look at early travel routes around Deadwood. Note how the road at upper left curves out of view much sooner than present-day Highway 85, using a different route over the hill.

In the modern view, the junction of Highways 85 (to Spearfish) and 14A (to Sturgis) lies at the upper center of the image. The rodeo grounds and football fields are visible at center left.

Field Note: This was a fun location to track down. I saw the background hills from elsewhere along this ridge, and eventually worked my way to the foreground. It is at the north end of White Rocks, away from where most people now climb to the summit. The Grizzly Gulch Fire of 2002 probably helped clear this site of trees that would otherwise have blocked at least part of the view.

Seeking a Fortune: Gold in the Hills

7-14-04 • N 44 22 33.9 W 103 43 38.7 • WEST

Circa 1885
"Deadwood Looking North"

Taken from within a few feet of the present-day flag pole at Mt. Moriah, this Pollock & Boyden view looks down into 1880s Deadwood. The unidentified man may be one of the photographers or an assistant. Snow is visible in the distance at upper left, and several buildings that survive from the 1880s can be found in both views.

Field Note: I have learned that you can't always believe what is written on an antique photo, no matter how original the information may seem to be. In this case, the scene shown is a view to the west, not north. This site view will be blocked by trees in a few years, barring a fire or tree thinning project above this part of Deadwood.

7-14-04 • N 44 22 33.0 W 103 43 38.8 • WEST

1879
"Deadwood After Fire"

The fire of 1879 burned much of the business section of Deadwood as well as many private homes, leaving behind this scene of devastation. The fire started in a bakery and spread to a hardware store, where kegs of gunpowder exploded and quickly spread the fire over a wide area of haphazardly built wooden structures.

There is some mystery about the purpose of the nearby flume (bottom); it may have carried water to a hydraulic mining operation in lower Whitewood Creek.

A foreground rock pinpoints this location precisely, although trees now block the view of town.

Field Note: The current photo was taken from just over the cliff edge south of the flag pole at Mt. Moriah, about 100 feet from the location at the facing page.

Circa 1902
Terraville, Gayville and Central City

Parts of three towns are visible in this undated photograph. On the hill at left is Terraville; at upper right is Central City; and in the foreground is the upper end of Gayville, including the Columbus Consolidated Mill.

The area was served by the Fremont, Elkhorn & Missouri Valley rail line (later the Chicago & Northwestern). The loop at bottom extended to Lead and was finished in 1902, one clue used in dating the image.

The Black Hills Yesterday & Today

9-14-05 • PRIVATE LAND • SOUTHWEST

Terraville has completely disappeared today, buried under waste rock from Homestake Mine's Open Cut. Historic excavations for rail lines and other activity can be glimpsed through trees in the modern scene, with the more recent Wharf Resources open pit mine visible in the distance at upper right.

Field Note: It is quite a hike to the ridge overlooking this area. The owner of the business at lower right told me he had hit several old steel rails while trying to dig near his building — probably some of the same rails visible in the historic photo, still present beneath the surface.

Seeking a Fortune: Gold in the Hills

9-15-05 • PRIVATE LAND • EAST

1876
"Gayville, or Troy"

This is one of many views recorded by photographer C.W. Stiff in the northern Black Hills around 1876. Some of the richest placer deposits were discovered in the area around Gayville (or Troy, a proposed alternate name). Stiff's images are so "early" that finding their present-day locations is extremely difficult.

The true site of Gayville seems to be in dispute among modern-day residents, but Stiff's title strongly points to this stretch of Highway 14A.

In the modern image, metal buildings have replaced rustic log miner's cabins. Overburden and waste rock from the Open Cut can be seen at extreme upper right.

Field Note: Tree growth and other changes made finding and matching the precise location a challenge. I clung to a steep hillside behind these businesses and eventually convinced myself I was "close enough" based on the shape of the middle and background hills.

9-15-05 • Private land • Southwest

Circa 1880
"Central City-Dakota"

Up the valley from Gayville, Central City had its own mining district and related industry. It was home to the Father DeSmet mine, upper left, acquired by Homestake in the 1880s.

The shape of the hills and of Central City's main street remain much the same, but Highway 14A has been added, and Homestake's Open Cut has removed the former location of the Father DeSmet mine.

Field Note: This location was used by several photographers for images of Central City in the 1880s and later. Tree growth required that I move a few feet closer and lower than the likely original site from which this image was taken.

1912
"Homestake Works, Lead, S.D."

This 1912 image by W.B. Perkins shows how the Open Cut, mine offices, milling plants, businesses and residential housing all co-existed in this area. For those who weren't there, it is hard to imagine how completely the Homestake Mine dominated the fabric and landscape of the town of Lead from the 19th Century to the 21st. Mining was given the highest priority, and over time almost everything seen here was moved or torn down to make way for the ever-expanding Open Cut.

The original Homestake claim was staked high on the hillside at center left.

9-14-05 • PRIVATE LAND • NORTHWEST

At first glance there isn't much here to tie this scene to the 1912 image, except a much larger Open Cut that has been dug to a depth of 800 feet. Closer examination reveals one surviving building: the light-colored structure at far right, which was built as an electrical substation in 1911. The rest of this part of town has disappeared over the years as the mine expanded.

Field Note: Early in this project, Dr. David Wolff directed my attention to the lone surviving building in the original photo. I chose the camera site based almost entirely on the angle of view of that building and the hillside above, which are nearly the only reference points left for re-creating the original view.

Circa 1935
Homestake Mine, Ore Processing Plant

Part of a postcard set of northern Black Hills scenes (another view is shown on the following spread), this image shows the ore processing facilities of Homestake Mining Company. There are also a number of homes on the hillside immediately adjacent to the industrial operations. A rail line, just visible at bottom, ran over to Central City, where it connected to other lines.

9-15-05 • Private land • Southeast

The roof of the home at bottom is one of the historic reference points in the modern scene. Much has changed across the valley, particularly after Homestake Mine ceased mining operations in 2002 and began dismantling their operation in Lead. But the foundations of the processing facility are still visible.

Another addition to the scene is the Yates Hoist, the tall white structure at upper center, which for years lowered miners and equipment down the shaft to a depth of 4,850 feet. This was only the first leg in a journey to the bottom of the mine, which reached nearly 8,000 feet. The Yates also hauled tons of gold ore back out of the earth.

Circa 1935

Homestake Mine, Ellison Hoist and Transformer Station

A companion to the postcard image on the preceding spread, this view from Washington Street looks out over a former electrical substation (lower right, the same one visible in the distance on pages 66-67). Across the way are the Ellison hoist, headframe, machine shops and, at right, part of the residential section of Lead.

9-15-05 • Private land • South

Many of the homes in the earlier photo have been moved or demolished as the Homestake's Open Cut expanded into the area (just visible at lower right). The mine closed down in 2002, but several mine buildings remain visible in the modern scene.

Circa 1900
Logging Camp at Elmore

Four men (including the one in white, who may have been a cook) pose stiffly for the unknown photographer. Elmore was a logging camp at the south end of Spearfish Canyon, probably shipping much of its output to the mines at Lead. Note the rail line at left, part of the Burlington & Missouri Railroad, which curves off-camera toward the photographer's position (a rail is visible in the lower left corner) and is also seen on the hill at far right.

The Black Hills Yesterday & Today

8-7-04 • Private land • North

It appears that a few of the same spruce trees survive in the same line behind a modern house that has been built in the area of present-day Elmore. The rail bed is now a gravel road, barely visible at left in this image.

Field Note: I stood on the former rail line for this matching image, though a bit lower than the original photographer. I believe he was shooting from a window or roof of the train.

Circa 1905
"Ragged Top Mountain. Camp of Cyanide and Mill."

The town of Cyanide was the home of the Spearfish Gold Mining and Reduction Company, which operated here from about 1902 to 1906, although it may have started several years earlier. The cyanide gold extraction method had been perfected about this time, making it possible to process this ore, though returns were apparently limited. Cyanide itself was once a good-sized town, seen here above the pile of mill tailings.

10-8-04 • Private Land • East

Ragged Top Mountain and the remains of the tailings pile are quite visible in the modern view, though all other signs of the town of Cyanide have been obliterated by time.

The general location of Cyanide and Ragged Top is between Terry Peak and the rim of Spearfish Canyon above Savoy. Some of the land in this vicinity is private property, mixed with Forest Service parcels.

Field Note: I could find no sign or remnant of the white foreground rocks in the historic image. They may have been buried in foliage nearby, but without that reference point this site only approximates the photographer's original location.

Seeking a Fortune: Gold in the Hills

7-16-05 • N 44 26 37.8 W 103 37 52.8 • Southwest

1877
Crook City

Oxen-powered freight wagons pause in the winter mud along the main street of Crook City, founded in 1876. The direction of the wagons suggests that they are outbound from the Hills, probably empty after delivering supplies for the settlers. The team in front is pulling four wagons connected together.

Named for well-known Army General George Crook, the town was later bypassed by the railroad in favor of Whitewood, only a mile away, which offered an easier grade for the roadbed. Crook City faded away after 1888.

Today the highway seems to overlay exactly the old muddy main street of Crook City.

Field Note: The snow-covered hill at the center of the historic image was used by at least two early photographers to record downtown Crook City, but trees now completely block these views.

7-16-05 • Private Land • Southwest

1878
"Crook City from the Northwest"

This is a relatively late image of Crook City. Photographer Stanley J. Morrow had visited here in 1876 or 1877 and documented the town under construction, but here it looks complete compared to the earlier images.

This particular stereoview is for some reason printed on card stock set up for a later series of flood images taken around Yankton, Morrow's home town. The date and title at left do not apply to this image.

Most if not all of the original buildings in Crook City are now long gone, replaced by modern housing and ranch buildings. Much of the town site is a private ranch, including the area from which this photo was taken.

Field Note: En route to this location (with permission of the landowner) I passed the site of the Crook City cemetery, where weathered gravestones further hint at the pioneer history of this area. At the photo site, I was relieved to find a clear view of the valley thanks to some recent logging.

Seeking a Fortune: Gold in the Hills

WHITEWOOD,
Black Hills, Dakota.
Northern or Black Hills Terminus for 1888, of the Fremont, Elkhorn & Missouri Valley R. R., situated in the beautiful Whitewood Valley, 10 miles b[...]
Photographed and Published by COULES & McBRIDE, Deadwood, Black Hills, Dakota.

Circa 1888

"Whitewood, Black Hills, Dakota."

Whitewood was established in 1887 by The Pioneer Townsite Company, a subsidiary of the Fremont, Elkhorn & Missouri Valley Railroad, which was building a line through the valley. This image is dated a year later.

7-15-05 • Private land • East

The camera site is on a high hill just west of downtown. Pine and oak trees have nearly blocked the formerly open view, but there are still glimpses of the rail line as well as the buildings that remain along Main Street.

Field Note: One of the fun things about visiting historic photo sites is recognizing something in the modern scene that is overlooked in the earlier image. Here I noticed Bear Butte's summit clearly visible in the distant upper left of the modern scene. This puzzled me until I studied the old photo again. Look carefully, and you will see Bear Butte there in the same place, though nearly lost in the faded sepia image.

Seeking a Fortune: Gold in the Hills

3-2-06 • N 43 55 40.9 W 103 34 36.4 • Northeast

1876
"Hill City."

Although someone had worked hard to start building the cabins and other structures seen in the historic view, there is no wood smoke or other sign of activity visible in the scene, even when examined under magnification. Perhaps this image was made during the period early in 1876 when Custer, Hill City and other mining venues were abandoned, after word spread of richer gold fields around Deadwood Gulch. In any case, this is one of the first images, if not the first, ever made of Hill City.

The modern viewpoint is probably within 25 feet of the original location. Construction of homes and streets around the site have leveled the former hillside, but the carefully matched background references point to this location half a block west of the south end of Main Street.

Field Note: I immediately recognized the unique hills in the distance of the historic photograph. They also appear (from another angle) in an image from the Custer Expedition of 1874. See pages 206-207 in *Exploring With Custer: The 1874 Black Hills Expedition*.

The Black Hills Yesterday & Today

4-28-06 • N 43 46 11.3 W 103 35 28.6 • West

1876
"Custer City."

This is one of the first images of Custer City, taken in early 1876 before winter snows had disappeared. Someone is home in the foreground cabins (note the wood smoke) while other crude homes are in various states of construction or abandonment. This may have been during the time when Custer (like Hill City, opposite page) was deserted by most of the population, who answered the call of new gold discoveries to the north.

The same ridges still run behind this formerly open meadow, although they are now covered by a forest of pine. Modern businesses and homes fill the valley, and one of Custer's school buildings is visible at upper center.

Field Note: Some massive earthwork has been done in recent years on the east side of Custer, where large apartment buildings have been built (off camera to the right of the modern image). Tree growth on the ridges is also hiding possible landscape clues. As a result, this image is an educated guess (within 100 yards) about the original location of the camera.

Seeking a Fortune: Gold in the Hills

Facing page: 10-3-03 • N 43 45 39.5 W 103 35 49.3 • Northwest

Circa 1885
"Birds eye view of a portion of Custer City looking north from Flag Rock"

The title of this view comes from a hand-written inscription on the back, apparently original to the unnamed photographer. Custer City, briefly named "Stonewall" in its earliest days, was founded in September 1875, making it the first official town in the Black Hills. Gen. Custer and his troops had camped in the valley a year earlier, when two practical miners with the Expedition discovered some gold here and larger quantities about three miles east.

Field Note: If you look closely, you can see that the foreground rock is actually several levels or shelves of granite. I was able to match the exact shape in the historic image only by placing my camera flat on the surface of this granite peak, as the earlier photographer must have done. Nearby, a neatly drilled hole may have been the base for a flagpole on "Flag Rock," a name that does not seem to survive in the present day.

9-19-05 • PRIVATE LAND • WEST

Circa 1890
"Reder Sawmill Southeast of Custer"

A note on the back of the historic photo says "Uncle Odo in Wagon." That would be Odo Reder, proprietor of the sawmill that stood where Sylvan Lake Road now runs, and the brother of the man who would go on to build the original lodge at Sylvan Lake in 1893. Perhaps some of the lumber in the historic scene is destined for that construction project a few miles up the road. The modern photo was taken from private property, very close to the original photo site. A man-made pond takes advantage of natural drainage through this valley.

1890

Building a Railroad

There is no information on the back of this image, but it would appear that these men and horses are working on the Burlington & Missouri River Railroad north of Custer. The line was completed to Deadwood in 1891.

Building a railroad line through the Hills was an important part of developing the interior towns. Several photographers recorded the construction in this area near Buckhorn Mountain.

The Black Hills Yesterday & Today

8-2-04 • N 43 47 49.8 W 103 37 22.0 • SOUTHEAST

The rail line was abandoned by the Burlington Railroad in the early 1980s, and eventually it became the Mickelson Trail, a hiking, biking and horseback-riding trail that runs the length of the Black Hills. The granite mass of Buckhorn Mountain towers over one of the prettiest sections of the trail.

Field Note: It is hard to believe how much dirt was filled in at this location — and along much of the rest of the line — to build up a level roadbed. I placed my camera exactly where the earlier photographer placed his, based on the alignment of rock formations in the background.

1891
"Harney Range, Horseshoe Curve on the B&M R'y near Custer City, S.D."

These mountains may be part of the "Harney Range," technically speaking, but the mountain itself is six miles away. In another of his images, photographer Grabill identified a rock a mile up the valley as "Harney Peak," so perhaps he was confused about the geography here.

This may have been one of the first runs of the Burlington & Missouri River Railroad into Custer. The line was completed to Deadwood in 1891, and the train seems to have been halted especially for the photographer in this scenic valley north of town.

8-2-04 • Vicinity: N 43 48 19.1 W 103 37 01.9 • North

With the advent of trucks and modern highways, along with a sharp decline in mining and milling operations, railroads began to disappear from the heart of the Black Hills. Only the remnants of roadbeds survive in many places, but the Burlington grade was developed for recreational use. Thousands of people enjoy the Mickelson Trail every year. The original camera point is on private land, though the trail itself (GPS reading) is public.

Circa 1885
Custer City

Many photographers took photos of Custer City from the high rocks south of town, but this is one of the earliest and clearest views of the arrangement of downtown buildings. The largest structure at left is the Custer County Courthouse, built in 1880-81. This image also gives us a sense of the "large grassed valley" described in a diary from the 1874 Custer Expedition, which camped here just a decade before this photo was made.

9-19-05 • N 43 45 40.9 W 103 36 05.9 • NORTHEAST

The "large grassed valley" of Gen. Custer's era is now dominated by brick, asphalt and all the colors of a modern town. Several 1880s Main Street buildings can still be picked out amid the development around them. Harney Peak and the Needles (upper right, in distance) still form a dramatic backdrop.

Field Note: If you look carefully at the alignment of the old Custer County Courthouse against the rock formations above it on Buckhorn Mountain, you will see I was forced to move a few feet to the left of the original camera point. A stand of pine trees now blocks the original view.

Seeking a Fortune: Gold in the Hills

Circa 1895

Main Street Custer, and Custer County Courthouse

The substantial structure at left served Custer County as a courthouse after it was completed in 1881. The construction dates are also known for several other buildings in the image, which help us date it to the mid-1890s. The main street of Custer (and other western towns) was wide enough for wagon masters to turn their bull teams.

The Black Hills Yesterday & Today

8-26-04 • N 43 45 57.2 W 103 36 07.4 • NORTHEAST

The old Courthouse, with brick additions on both ends, continues to stand watch over Main Street. The building now houses the 1881 Courthouse Museum, operated by the Custer County Historical Society. Several other buildings in the historic image can also be seen in the modern view of this bustling little town.

Field Note: Although the street scene looks quiet enough here, I had to dodge across the street every time a stoplight in the next block turned red, giving me another few seconds to try to shoot a matching image. I suspect this was a problem not encountered by the earlier photographer!

8-25-04 • N 43 45 32.1 W 103 37 33.3 • North

1876
"Bear Rock, Miner's Cabin in Foreground"

Bear Rock was one of the benchmarks used to record mining claims around Custer during the early months of the gold rush. Morrow apparently recorded this view while he was in the vicinity taking photos of Gen. Crook's troops, some of whom were camped nearby (see page 39).

A historic marker notes the significance of Bear Rock, and hides part of a sculpture from an art studio that was nearby when the modern view was taken.

Bear Rock can easily be seen from Highway 16A on the west edge of Custer.

Field Note: Local residents say some part of this rock does look like a bear, but I couldn't see it, from this angle at least.

8-11-04 • Private land • North

Circa 1882
Hot Springs

Annie Tallent's book (see bibliography) says this was the first house built on the town site of Hot Springs, constructed by Dr. R.A. Stewart. The town site was laid out in December 1882 (apparently receiving its current name in 1883), and the home served as a stage stop and hotel.

Note the horses and wagons posed in the middle of Fall River, as well as the small footbridge in the foreground.

Remnants of its past are still visible in the graceful 1890s homes on the ridge and in the sandstone buildings along Fall River.

Field Note: I eventually learned that this photo site, a hill with a good view looking up North River Street, was used by numerous photographers over the years. Trees are now blocking much of the view, but there are still a couple of "windows" through the branches, as seen here.

Circa 1900
"Etta Tin Mine Mill & U.S. Monument Rock," Keystone

The Etta Tin Mine opened in 1883, and the mill (shown here) was built later in the decade. Not much tin was ever produced, although this fact was kept from investors over the years. The mine would later be known for its pegmatite. Note the two women perched atop Monument Rock. They are not identified on the original photo.

7-8-04 • N 43 53 09.1 W 103 25 18.2 • South

The foundations of the mill can still be found in the woods above the present-day recreational vehicle parking area, but the building has been torn down.

Note that the bottom of Monument Rock has been buried to a depth of several feet above its original base.

Circa 1930

Holy Terror Mine at Keystone

The town of Keystone was named for a mine discovered in 1891. Nearby, the Holy Terror Mine (above, named somewhat in jest for the wife of the man who staked the claim) was opened in 1894. It produced large quantities of gold and helped the town boom for a number of years. It was eventually connected to the Keystone Mine by underground shafts.

6-8-05 • Vicinity N 43 53 54.4 W 103 25 06.4 • North

Several of the original Holy Terror Mine buildings still stand on the hillside above historic "old" Keystone. In some ways the town represents the history of the Black Hills, with its transition from mining to tourism.

Field Note: You can see the Holy Terror by turning east on Highway 40 at the stoplight in Keystone and driving a few blocks (the GPS reading is for the side of the road across from the mine). Old Keystone is an interesting part of town away from the tourist strip that leads to Mt. Rushmore. The Keystone Area Historical Society operates a museum in the old Keystone Schoolhouse in this part of town.

Seeking a Fortune: Gold in the Hills

8-7-04 • N 43 57 44.82 W 103 36 16.0 • SOUTHEAST

Circa 1885
"Newton Fork."

Newton Fork was named after geologist Henry Newton, one of the leaders of the 1875 Expedition that continued assessing and mapping the Black Hills after Custer's discovery of gold a year earlier. An 1884 map calls this creek "Newton Fork," and a man-made lake further down the valley is also named after the explorer.

A wagon in the middle distance probably belongs to the photographers, and it appears that a wagon trail is being established in the valley. Harney Peak is visible on the horizon at right, while in the modern view the Deerfield Road as well as the Mickelson Trail now pass through "Newton Fork."

Field Note: I had fun tracking this one down. I recognized Harney Peak as well as the view from this general direction northwest of Hill City. A fireman I spoke with in town recognized the name "Newton Fork" and said it was up the Deerfield Road. After a short drive by car and a ride up the trail by bike, I located the site.

The Black Hills Yesterday & Today

9-8-05 • Private land • East

1878
"Bear Butte Camp Sturgis"

This view of Camp J.G. Sturgis was taken sometime after July 18, 1878, when the 7th Cavalry set up a temporary base for a few weeks while a site for a permanent Army fort could be selected. Construction on Ft. Meade started later that fall, just a few miles from this location.

The camp was named for the son of Col. Samuel D. Sturgis, who died with Custer at the Little Big Horn in 1876. Col. Sturgis commanded the 7th Cavalry following Custer's death. The site today is a pasture on private property.

Seeking a Fortune: Gold in the Hills

9-8-05 • N 44 24 52.2 W 103 30 36.2 • West

Circa 1880
Freight Wagons, Sturgis

The town of Sturgis grew to prominence thanks to its proximity to Ft. Meade, the military post established a few miles to the east in 1878. Sturgis was also near a crossroads of stage and freight roads from Sidney, Ft. Pierre and Bismark, a fact which explains the activity in the historic photo.

Main Street today bears little resemblance to the original scene, with no sign of the original wooden buildings. Background hills confirm that this view is looking the right direction, however.

Seeking a Fortune: Gold in the Hills

1888
Comanche at Ft. Meade

Comanche was found on the Little Big Horn battlefield after Custer's defeat in 1876, so severely injured that some of the soldiers who found him felt he should be dispatched immediately. Sgt. Korn (pictured here) objected when he recognized the horse as belonging to one of the fallen officers in Custer's command. He nursed the horse back to health with help from other men.

Comanche was brought to Ft. Meade, where the commander gave Korn the duty of caring for the horse and ordered that he should never again carry an "earthly rider."

The back of this photo contains Korn's account of the battle along with his story of saving Comanche.

The Black Hills Yesterday & Today

8-3-04 • N 44 24 27.5 W 103 28 40.9 • NORTHWEST

The field where Sgt. Korn once posed with Comanche lies just outside the main housing area of Ft. Meade, which was established east of Sturgis as a cavalry post in 1878. Several surviving buildings are visible against the backdrop of Bear Butte.

Ft. Meade now serves as a center for the Veteran's Administration hospital and related facilities. Also located here is the Ft. Meade Cavalry Museum, with numerous exhibits about the history of this frontier post.

Field Note: I originally had little faith that I would be able to find this site. As with other sites in the book, however, locating the background (Bear Butte and Ft. Meade) led to finding the foreground. Horses still graze this pasture, though they were off-camera when I made my photo.

Circa 1906
Fort Meade

A buggy, presumably belonging to the photographer, is parked in the foreground on a hill just south of Ft. Meade. Bear Butte, a popular landmark and reference point, rises about five miles to the northeast.

The fort was home to the 7th Cavalry for many years after it was built in 1878. The substantial brick and wooden buildings seen here were added as officer quarters and barracks in following years.

8-2-04 • N 44 24 21.5 W 103 28 32.3 • North

Although some of the wooden buildings have been modified or removed over the past century, a number of the original brick buildings can still be seen through the trees around the parade ground of Ft. Meade.

Also compare the small white hill on the horizon, to the right of Bear Butte, with its counterpart in the historic image. This is the site of a quarry that has considerably reduced the size of the hill over time.

The white buildings partially visible at right are part of the Veteran's Administration facility, which opened here during World War II.

Field Note: The alignment of buildings with the background points to this rise as the original photo site, though I did move to an adjacent area clear of foreground trees. There has been some excavation on this hilltop; note the depressions in the foreground.

1877

Rapid City

With the "artist dark room in foreground," according to a notation on the back of this stereoview, Stanley Morrow recorded a then-distant view of Rapid City when it was little more than a year old.

The foreground ravine and hillside remain virtually unchanged today, but the city has engulfed the camera point and grown well beyond it in all directions.

Field Note: This site is on private property at the west edge of present-day Star Village. The reference to the Great Flood at Yankton on the side of the stereocard is for another set of photos by Stanley J. Morrow.

The Black Hills Yesterday & Today

5-4-05 • N 44 04 53.8 W 103 13 51.1 • West

1878
Rapid City

Rapid City was sometimes called "Hay Camp" in the early days, due to the wide plain west of the original town site. In this photo, a hay wagon appears to be bringing a load back through "the Gap" carved by Rapid Creek in the background.

The reverse side of this stereoview lists several names, some of whom may have been the people in the photograph. The names are Orpha L. Haxby, Mattie Lewis, Elda Chase, Geo. Chase, Dan Gitchell and Wm. Lewis.

Another notation on the back reads "West St. Joe St., Rapid City, S.D. 1878." Since South Dakota wouldn't become a state until 1889, the notation was clearly written much later. The photo site aligns more closely with West Main, near the intersection of Mt. Rushmore Road.

Field Note: Although this was a difficult site to identify precisely, the ridge at upper right (present-day "M Hill") and the sandstone outcropping below it served as good reference points. Moving more than a short distance from this location threw the reference points out of alignment, it seemed to me. Other researchers believe the site is up to two blocks west of here.

Seeking a Fortune: Gold in the Hills

Circa 1885
"Rapid City, Black Hills, D.T."

This view is from a lower shoulder of Hangman's Hill, looking east-northeast into downtown Rapid City over the top of a water reservoir built in 1885. According to historian Carl H. Leedy, the reservoir was fed by gravity from nearby City Springs and held 375,986 gallons at an elevation of 188 feet above Main Street.

John R. Brennan and George Stokes used a compass and tape measure to mark the original square-mile town site of Rapid City on Feb. 25, 1876. The Journey Museum now houses a wonderful collection of exhibits covering the geology, archaeology and history — both white and Native American — of this valley and the Black Hills.

4-28-06 • N 44 04 41.5 W 103 14 33.3 • East

Modern Rapid City has sprawled far beyond its early boundaries on Rapid Creek. The photo site, originally several blocks from the edge of town, is now surrounded by homes about 150 yards below the present-day Dinosaur Hill gift shop. The shelf where the reservoir once stood now provides room for a curve on Skyline Drive.

Field Note: It was only by looking at photographs taken *of* early-day Hangman's Hill (rather than *from* it) that I was able to spot the location of the former reservoir. Once I realized that the circular roadbed had been the base of the reservoir, the pieces came together.

Circa 1885
Evans Transportation Line, Rapid City

A wagon at right bears the legend "Evans Transportation Line," referring to the well-known Black Hills freighter Fred Evans. Apparently on its way to Black Hills settlements, the train has stopped here in "the Gap" just west of downtown. Among the men standing in the foreground are two on either side of a large camera, possibly part of the team that made this image using another camera.

A bank of Rapid Creek is visible at right.

5-20-05 • N 44 04 55.4 W 103 14 27.0 • NORTH

West Main Street in the Gap is today a busy four-lane road, one of two arteries carrying virtually all traffic between downtown and West Rapid City. In pioneer times this was called the Gateway to the Black Hills.

The foreground of the historic photo, where wagon trains once rolled, is now a commercial and industrial area. On M Hill is one of the many transmission towers on the "hogback" that surrounds much of the Hills.

Field Note: This is another site that is difficult to pinpoint precisely. The few foreground clues in the landscape are now buried under roads or buildings, but the sandstone cliffs, aligned with the hill in the background, point to this vicinity.

Circa 1889

"Rapid City, D.T., 8th Cavalry in distance, Black Hills."

Looking north from behind and above the first Rapid City high school, this view provides another glimpse of the town's early days. The numbers were written on the photograph by an early owner to identify certain homes and businesses. According to the original caption, the tents on a distant bluff are an encampment of the 8th Cavalry.

8-28-06 • N 44 04 30.1 W 103 13 47.1 • NORTH

Except for the land itself, very little remains from the days of Dakota Territory. Only one or two buildings are still visible at center, in the heart of downtown.

The building at far left, under the large American flag, was formerly a depot and warehouse for the Crouch Line, a railroad that used to run from Rapid City to Mystic. Dakota Middle School now stands in the foreground, constructed around an earlier structure that once stood adjacent to the original school.

Field Note: Sorting out which school building stood where (and when) in the foreground of the historic image — and correlating that to the modern view — proved to be a surprisingly complicated task requiring several visits to this site. With help from Reid Riner at the Minnilusa Pioneer Museum, I was finally able to narrow down the location to very near this spot.

Circa 1900
"Cambria, Wyoming, on the B.&M. R.R."

An early view of Cambria, Wyoming, reveals the extent of this mining complex. Coal was discovered here in 1887 and mined until it ran out in 1928.

The mine and the town both closed virtually overnight. It is said that the town was abandoned so hastily by people worried about finding jobs elsewhere that, years later, cards still lay on the tables in the local pool hall and pots still sat on stoves in some of the homes.

9-27-05 • Private land • South

The valley has now returned to nature except for the remnants of waste piles, debris and even some of the streets through town.

The former site of Cambria is a remote, privately owned valley about seven miles north of Newcastle.

Field Note: The owners of the Cambria site kindly transported me here by ATV, at times following the old rail line. (Wooden ties were still visible along much of the route.) Please respect their property rights and do not venture here without permission.

Seeking a Fortune: Gold in the Hills

Cambria upper end of canyon

1901
Cambria, WY

Neat but nearly identical homes line this residential street in the middle of Cambria, a true "company town" served by churches and schools as long as the nearby coal mine was in operation.

Timber has nearly been cleared from the surrounding hillsides, no doubt for construction of these buildings or for use in the mine.

9-27-05 • Private land • North

Walking through this valley now, it is hard to imagine the activity that once took place here. One or two structures and numerous foundations are about all that is left along the once picturesque street, and a cemetery above the former town reminds visitors about the people who once lived here. The forest, meanwhile, is regenerating and nearly blocks the view up the "street" that once ran through Cambria. The former town site is now private property.

Building Towns & Cities

The railroad reached Custer in 1890 and was completed all the way to Deadwood by the following year, signaling a new era in the Black Hills. Wagon trains, stagecoaches and other trappings of pioneer times began to disappear from daily use, relegated to museums and history books. There were still occasional gold or other mineral discoveries and much of the economy continued to center on mining activity. But the towns and cities of the Black Hills were also expanding their economies and preparing to enter a new century.

April 10, 1924
Flood at Belle Fourche

The Goddess of Justice looks out over an alarming scene as floodwaters from the Belle Fourche River lap at the street across from the Butte County Courthouse, where this photograph was taken from the roof. In the distance are the Belle Fourche rodeo grounds, with grandstands and a surrounding fence rising above the floodwaters.

5-6-06 • N 44 40 07.1 W 103 51 12.1 • West

Justice has raised her sword in this modern image, a change that was apparently made during a recent restoration project. But she continues to gaze out toward the horizon from her perch on the courthouse roof in the town of Belle Fourche.

A service station and a home have been built in the intervening years across Highway 85 from the courthouse, and new trees have grown up to replace some of those possibly lost in the flood — although a few appear to have survived in the modern view.

Field Note: On the following page you can see the window in the courthouse cupola from which the historic photo was taken. The window is now boarded up and unusable. I recreated the image by climbing out on the roof, hoisting my camera on a tripod to the level of the window, and firing the shutter with a remote control — without looking through the viewfinder. This was a situation in which using a digital camera provided a clear advantage, allowing me to review each attempt until I had the image I wanted. Even so, it took a while to align the shot properly.

7-15-05 • Vicinity N 44 40 06.6 W 103 51 13.0 • East

1911
Dedication of Courthouse, Belle Fourche

The Butte County Courthouse (facing page) was dedicated following its construction in 1911. Note the window in the center of the cupola, described as a camera location on the previous spread. In the foreground is a flume that carried water to a nearby flour mill.

Today the courthouse still serves the residents of Butte County, with the help of wings that were later added on each side to accommodate more office space.

Field Note: I backed up as far as I could for this image, to the front wall of the service station that is now across from the courthouse. The historic camera location was probably a few feet further back on a site now covered by the building.

Building Towns & Cities

7-15-05 • N 44 40 16.8 W 103 51 13.4 • NORTHEAST

Circa 1910

"Main Streets of Belle Fourche, S.D."

An oversize colorized postcard (top) offers a panoramic view of downtown Belle Fourche at the intersection of 5th and State Streets. Today, 5th is also known as Highway 85. Belle Fourche was originally a cattle town, platted along the railroad line in 1891. For many years it was the largest cattle shipping point in the country.

Field Note: The bottom image was carefully combined from several photos I took at this site, the only place in the book where I did this type of digital retouching. Be sure to visit the Tri-State Museum a few blocks up 5th Street to the left.

202 Diversion Dam, Belle Fourche, S. D.

7-14-05 • N 44 44 12.4 W 103 40 28.4 • East

Circa 1920
"Diversion Dam, Belle Fourche, S.D."

Construction began in 1905 on the Belle Fourche Dam (also known as Orman Dam) and was completed in 1914, about eight miles northeast of Belle Fourche. At 6,262 feet long and 122 feet high, it was the largest earthen dam of its kind at that time.

The historic view was taken from the top of the dam looking at the discharge area downstream.

The reservoir now supplies water for irrigating some 57,000 acres of cropland. The road in the modern view provides access to nearby beaches and fishing areas.

Circa 1925
"Main St. Newell"

Newell was born as a planned headquarters for the Belle Fourche Irrigation Project, which would build Orman Dam across Owl Creek a few miles away (see preceding page). Chief Engineer Frederick Haynes Newell inspected the "government town site" as it was platted in 1907, and by 1909 settlers were building a nearby shanty town even before this site was officially laid out.

7-14-05 • N 44 42 52.9 W 103 25 13.9 • North

Newell's main street is officially named Girard Avenue, but everyone seems to call it "Main." The brick building on the corner at left is still in use, and some of its wooden neighbors may also date to 1925 or earlier, but those on the other side of the street have been replaced. The history of the town and surrounding area is preserved at the Newell Museum, located just a half-block west of this camera location.

Field Note: I have nearly been run over by cars several times while trying to rephotograph Main Streets in other towns, but this was the closest I ever came to getting run over by farm machinery.

Circa 1930

"City of Newell, S.D. from Water Tower"

Newell was incorporated in 1910. A post office was also established that year, as was rail service, and a public school was completed in 1911. Once the streets had been marked and named, settlers in the shanty town began moving their buildings to the new site.

An intrepid photographer climbed the town's water tower about 1930 to record this overview.

11-1-05 • N 44 42 56.5 W 103 25 40.7 • SOUTHEAST

Even though the historic photo was taken in a season when there were no leaves on the trees, it is easy to see how those trees have grown. Several buildings are visible in both images, most notably the church at far right.

Newell is the center of a varied agricultural community and ships thousands of sheep every year through the local sale yard.

Field Note: There was little question about where this historic image was taken! Wearing a safety harness, I climbed the rungs of the ladder on one side of the water tower, dislodging a few pigeons (and their debris) on the way up. I was glad to reach the ground safely again. Though well-built, the water tower is at least 75 years old and a bit rusty in places.

Spearfish in Territorial Days

Circa 1885
"Spearfish, Dakota"

Spearfish shines at sunset in a rare early image, taken before statehood in 1889. Founded in 1876, the town was established by people who originally intended to look for gold, but instead were attracted by the agricultural possibilities of this fertile, well-watered valley.

The Black Hills Yesterday & Today

6-2-05 • Private Land • Northeast

Spearfish still shines, here with a coat of new spring green. Also clearly visible are the colors of the rock formations rising toward Lookout Mountain (off camera to the right). This view was taken near the present-day Passion Play amphitheater.

Field Note: The owners of the Black Hills Passion Play kindly let me roam their property seeking and eventually locating this site. It was amazing to see at last those same little knolls in the foreground as well as a fence line in about the same position as the 1880s fence.

Circa 1890
"Sturgis, S.D."

There is one problem with information written on old photos: it isn't necessarily accurate. In this case, someone has written the apparently authoritative inscription "Sturgis" on a view of Spearfish. The open avenue at right is present-day Kansas Street, while Jackson Boulevard is the next street to the left.

8-7-04 • Private Land • West

Over the years, several photographers have taken advantage of this hill on the north side of town, just off the present-day Jackson Boulevard exit from Interstate 90, to record views of Spearfish and distant Crow Peak.

The foreground has been quarried, and a motel has replaced the barn and cow pen that once existed below the hill. Like other Black Hills towns, Spearfish has long since grown past the boundaries established by its founders.

Field Note: I had hoped to find some of the rocks in the foreground of the historic image, but the surface seems to have been quarried out, leaving the depression or gully seen in the modern photo.

Circa 1895
Spearfish Stage

The Spearfish coach is ready for the haul to Deadwood, its likely destination, while passengers wait for the unknown photographer to record this image against the backdrop of Lookout Mountain.

The Spearfish stage ran until 1913, when auto travel finally made it obsolete. Harvey Fellows was the driver of this stage for more than three decades and may well be one of the men at the reins.

4-15-05 • N 44 29 09.1 W 103 51 23.1 • NORTHEAST

This neighborhood at Seventh and Elgin Streets is just south of historic downtown Spearfish, which fits well with the historic image of a coach ready to depart from what was then the edge of town.

Field Note: I worked for several hours to assure myself that landforms seen in the historic photo, now hidden behind the trees in the distance, were indeed lined up. These were the clues that led me to this spot, which I believe is no more than 50 feet from the original camera point.

Facing Page: 8-14-04 • N 44 22 36.2 W 103 43 13.2 • Southwest

Circa 1900
Deadwood from White Rocks

White Rocks was a popular place for recording early images of Deadwood Gulch, but few of them show the "lay of the land" as clearly as this view from about 1900, looking over Mt. Moriah cemetery toward the center of town.

Specific clues provided by the foreground rocks make it possible to pinpoint the location of the original photographer's tripod on the edge of the formation. Several historic buildings are still visible in the modern image, but this is another situation where tree growth has obscured much of the original view.

Field Note: It is a strenuous but pleasant hike from Mt. Moriah Cemetery to the top of White Rocks, with spectacular views in all directions. From here you can barely hear the music and casino barkers far below on Main Street.

1908
"Chicago & North Western Depot, Deadwood, S.D."

The C. & N.W. line (originally built as the Fremont, Elkhorn & Missouri Valley Railroad) reached Deadwood in December 1890, and the depot was built in 1897. This dated postcard provides a view of the cliffs below Mt. Moriah, which in earlier times were festooned with billboards and graffiti.

6-22-05 • N 44 22 31.8 W 103 43 50.4 • East

The former depot served as City Hall from 1952 to 1991. Since then it has housed the Deadwood visitor center. Fully restored to its former glory, it is a gem of the downtown area. Behind it are Deadwood's post office and the bell tower of the Adams Museum.

Field Note: When you go to Deadwood, be sure to stop at the Adams Museum behind the depot. It is a treasure trove of Deadwood history that could easily occupy a few hours.

Building Towns & Cities

Circa 1895
Elizabethtown, Deadwood

Elizabethtown was originally a separate mining camp in the lower end of Deadwood Gulch, north of the town that would eventually grow large enough to absorb.

This view can be dated to the post-1890 era, when a rail line began operating to Whitewood. The large white spots are damaged areas on the original photograph.

The Black Hills Yesterday & Today

7-12-04 • Private Land • Northwest

A few 19th-century houses still survive near the intersection of Burnham Avenue and Highway 85/14A, but many buildings in the earlier image have disappeared. Whitewood Creek has also been rechanneled, its far bank just visible at bottom, and the cliff known locally as Brown Rocks now wears a thicker coat of pine trees.

1888

"Ingleside, Deadwood"

Ingleside (occasionally spelled Engleside) included the site of Deadwood's original cemetery, but level space has always been a premium in this mountain gulch. The cemetery was moved up to the steeper slopes of Mt. Moriah around 1877, freeing the area for the construction of fashionable homes in the late 1800s. This view was taken not long before the railroad came through this part of town. Note White Rocks at upper left. The white specks scattered across the hillside are tree stumps.

7-21-04 • Private Land • Northeast

Ingleside remains a residential neighborhood of many now-historic homes, including the Adams House, which is fully restored and open to the public. The growth of deciduous trees in yards and along the streets now hides some of those homes from the camera.

Field Note: The hillside at this photo site is very steep, not an obvious place to set up a tripod-mounted camera. Part of the hill may have been mined in the past, or removed for other reasons, but it does seem to be very close to the original camera position.

Facing Page: 3-31-04 • N 44 22 35.5 W 103 43 13.8 • Southwest

Circa 1905
"Deadwood from White Rocks"

This is one of the many scenic images recorded near White Rocks above Deadwood. In this case the direction is southwest, across McGovern Hill.

Today the view includes the pile of waste rock taken from the Open Cut (the wide green area in the center); the ski runs on Terry Peak (the highest distant peak); and the surface mines of the Golden Reward and Wharf Resources (brown areas to the right of Terry Peak).

Building Towns & Cities

Circa 1900

"Deadwood, S.D. on the B.&M. R.R."

Offering this view of downtown Deadwood, McGovern Hill was easily reached and often used by photographers over the years. The original Deadwood High School, built in 1899, is prominent at left.

3-31-04 • Private Land • Northeast

The Lead-Deadwood Elementary School now stands on the site of the old high school, but numerous buildings and homes are visible in both images. The distant ridge is nearly devoid of trees, burned off in the fire of 1959.

Field Note: Because of tree growth and the construction of water tanks (which leveled a large area of hillside used by the earlier photographer) I was not able to shoot from the precise historic location, which is perhaps 100 feet away.

August, 1920
Pactola

Originally a mining camp with a hotel and stage stop, Pactola was first called Camp Crook. Like Crook City, it was named for the Army general who came to the Black Hills in 1875 and again in 1876, leading the "Starvation March." During the Prohibition era of the 1920s this area was known as "the valley of a thousand smokes," referring to the fires of illegal whiskey stills.

Pactola was the center of a ranching and recreation area for most of its pre-reservoir existence, home to bible camps, family vacation cabins and the famous Moosecamp Lodge. This early photo preserves a view of an unidentified ranch and the rails of the Crouch Line, which ran from Rapid City to Mystic via Pactola.

The Black Hills Yesterday & Today

7-9-05 • N 44 04 01.7 W 103 29 06.7 • West

The Bureau of Land Reclamation contracted to build a dam across Rapid Creek beginning in 1953. By 1958 the reservoir was full, providing water for Rapid City and Rapid Valley. Pactola's history lives on, however, in archives and photo books at the Black Hills National Forest Visitor Center on Highway 385, overlooking the now-flooded valley.

Field Note: This is one of my favorite locations of the entire project. I was astonished and excited to see the background hills rising in the distance, just as in the historic image. As if on cue, the waterskier came by after I had set up my camera at the photo site.

Circa 1920
Sheridan

An early gold camp and the original Pennington County seat, Sheridan was founded in a valley along Spring Creek between Hill City and Pactola. This wintery scene was taken from a high hill south of the town.

The Black Hills Yesterday & Today

3-15-06 • N 43 58 47.2 W 103 28 05.4 • SOUTHWEST

Sheridan is remembered today in the name of the lake that covers the town site. The remains of the original road into town can be glimpsed at center right, now terminating at a beach. Highway 385 runs along the west side of the lake.

Field Note: I tried to time my arrival at this location to match incoming winter weather. There are very few historic images of Sheridan in Black Hills archives. If you know of any, please let me know.

Facing page: 7-9-05 • N 44 07 17.2 W 103 42 34.7 • South

October 1914
Rochford Station

In this image from a personal photo album, a train rolls toward a depot about two miles below the early mining town of Rochford. The Chicago, Burlington & Quincy Railroad arrived here in 1890.

Today (facing page), the rail line is part of the Mickelson Trail, visible through the trees at lower right, and gravel roads have replaced the rails as the primary means of transportation.

June, 1914
"Standby House" near Rochford

This image was taken from the ore dump of the well-known Standby Mine about half a mile below Rochford. What the photographer called "Standby House" was apparently the home of the mine manager.

The mine was located in 1877, operating intermittently over the years and as late as the 1930s. The Burlington rail line curves through the scene between the home and the mine.

The Black Hills Yesterday & Today

7-9-05 • N 44 07 15.6 W 103 42 36.7 • NORTHEAST

Only broken glass and a few rocks mark the location of the old house, and bikers on a day trip ride the Mickelson Trail where trains once rode the rails. The Rochford Road is visible at upper left and in the middle distance.

Field Note: At this writing the area of the Standby Mine (where this photo was taken from) may soon be closed to the public. Use caution if you find your way here as there are numerous hazards. The GPS reading is for the Mickelson Trail, from where you can view the mine area safely.

1919
"View S.W. from Cowboy Hill, Rapid City, S.D."

In 1919 Rapid City had not yet expanded west through "the Gap" in the hogback ridge that surrounds most of the Black Hills. This fine view of largely undeveloped land was preserved by the energetic J. Harlan Johnson, whose work was found in well-organized personal albums. Several of his photographs appear in this book.

The dammed or dredged area along Rapid Creek in the foreground may have been associated with Warren Lamb Lumber Company, which was located nearby. The complex in the middle distance is the Rapid City Indian School, which was still operating at the time. Harney Peak is just visible in the distant haze on the horizon.

8-17-05 • N 44 05 15.7 W 103 15 03.1 • SOUTHWEST

The former open fields of West Rapid are now an area of homes and businesses, and the old Indian school has been converted to a medical facility called Sioux San or Rapid City Indian Hospital (note the water tower).

Most of the park land here owes its existence to the devastating flood of 1972, after which the city established a greenway in the Rapid Creek floodplain.

Field Note: It was a pleasant experience to find a photograph so clearly and accurately captioned with date and location. It was an equally pleasant hike to the near-summit of Cowboy Hill (now generally called "M Hill") to examine the changes in the view since 1919.

Circa 1915
Rapid City, Looking Northwest

This view from a hillside above South Street, a boundary of the original town site, looks out over what was then the western edge of Rapid City. To the left of the Gap is Hangman's Hill.

On the right, Cowboy Hill is already marked by the 'M' that was placed in 1911, the earliest possible date for this image. Since there are no automobiles visible anywhere, it is also likely that the photo was taken not too long *after* 1911.

The Black Hills Yesterday & Today

4-28-06 • N 44 04 30.8 W 103 13 49.2 • NORTHWEST

Several homes are common to both images, at least one of them converted to business use on Mt. Rushmore Road (mid-photo), which is now a busy thoroughfare funneling traffic into the Black Hills. The 'M' on the distant hill has remained in precisely the same location, with the addition of an 'S' and 'D' on either side.

Forest cover has expanded on both M and Hangman's Hills, as well as the foothills beyond.

Field Note: The unknown photographer shot his view from about a third of the way down the hill from present-day Hillcrest Drive, rather than from the easily-approached summit. Perhaps it was a compositional decision, to feature the foreground homes more prominently.

9-23-05 • N 44 04 52.8 W 103 13 45.0 • East

Circa 1904

"Indian Pony Races, Stockman's Day, Rapid City, S.D."

Stockmen's Day (facing page) was a highlight of the calendar each April from 1898-1910, a period when stock raising was even more central to the economy than it is today. The event was an opportunity for ranchers to socialize with each other and with cattle buyers.

The historic view, taken during Indian Pony Races at 7th and Main in downtown Rapid City, reveals just how much things have changed. Only the present-day Prairie Edge building at the far end of the block survives — and horses no longer race on the paved streets of downtown.

Indian Pony Race.
Stockmans Day Rapid City S.D.

Circa 1895 (July 4)
Sturgis Main Street, Looking Northwest

The prominent display of American flags and celebrating crowds make it likely that this is a 4th of July celebration. But the original photograph carries no date or any information about the race being run on Main Street. Several members of the Cavalry from Ft. Meade watch the action from horseback at right.

The Black Hills Yesterday & Today

8-9-04 • N 44 24 51.5 W 103 30 36.5 • Northwest

Sturgis has today become famous for its huge motorcycle rally held each August. Initiated in 1938, the event has grown from a gathering of a few enthusiasts to a flood of more than 500,000 bikers in peak years.

Field Note: My thanks to the owner of the building which houses the Dungeon Bar and Rushmore Office Supplies for letting me up on the roof during the height of the motorcycle rally. The GPS reading is for the street level below.

Circa 1890
Sturgis Main Street, Looking East

The Main Street of Sturgis is astir with horses, wagons and people in a scene from the late 1800s. The town not only supplied nearby Ft. Meade with food and forage, it provided a popular marketplace for local farms and ranches. All this trading activity helped Sturgis boom during the period.

The Black Hills Yesterday & Today

8-9-04 • N 44 24 52.3 W 103 30 42.5 • East

Another view of Sturgis during the peak of the annual motorcycle rally contrasts chrome and steel against the horse-drawn wooden wagons that once operated here.

Some of the same buildings may be visible in both scenes, but the lack of clarity in the historic image makes it difficult to be certain.

Field Note: I am most appreciative that the owners of Tom's T's granted me access to their balcony for this image during the Rally.

Facing Page: 9-7-05 • Private Land • South

Circa 1900
Sturgis, S.D.

The ridge just south of downtown once provided a panoramic view of Sturgis. Tree growth now obscures much of that view, and blocks it completely where the early photographer probably set up his camera. The modern image was made about 50 feet from the original site.

Field Note: With help from a nearby landowner, I was able to navigate a trail to the top of the ridge by car, then travel on foot to the photo site. I arrived just in time for the sunset image I had sought.

Circa 1890
"Main Street, Hill City, Looking South"

Several Main Street buildings are under construction in this 1890s view. Prominent at right is the Harney Peak Hotel, headquarters of the Harney Peak Tin Company, which operated for many years. The company was essentially an investment scheme, never producing any significant quantity of tin. But it did bring prosperity to Hill City with construction of the hotel, a mill and company offices, employing many people.

The Black Hills Yesterday & Today

9-21-05 • N 43 56 00.2 W 103 34 31.3 • SOUTH

Hill City's Main Street is active and prosperous today, especially during the summer months when it draws visitors to the many shops, restaurants and art galleries. The former Harney Peak Tin Company building (at right) is now a popular place to dine.

Field Note: Immediately off-camera to the right is the Black Hills Institute of Geological Research, including a museum with a fantastic collection of minerals, fossils and more — including dinosaurs!

171

Circa 1933
Main St. Hill City, S.D.

By the 1930s, Hill City was already promoting itself as a tourist destination with a version of the slogan that is still in use today ("Heart of the Hills"). There are at least four gas stations visible in this picture postcard, waiting to serve the Model A cars passing through, and AAA advertises its services on the roof of a building at left. This view is looking south up Main Street.

The Black Hills Yesterday & Today

9-21-05 • N 43 56 05.3 W 103 34 30.6 • SOUTH

Good fortune would smile on Hill City with the carving of Crazy Horse Memorial and Mt. Rushmore National Memorial nearby. The two attractions draw visitors from all over the world, many of whom come through town. Several buildings can be seen in both images, and there are still plenty of gas stations.

Field Note: I was delighted to find this view not blocked by trees, as was a similar nearby view by the same photographer.

Circa 1930
"Tourist Camp Hill City, S.D."

With the advent of a Black Hills visitor industry, tourist camps like this one sprang up near most of the principal towns. This one isn't drawing much interest yet.

This view of Hill City was taken from a hill to the east of Main Street.

The Black Hills Yesterday & Today

9-21-05 • PRIVATE LAND • WEST

Hill City is one of the quintessential Black Hills towns, having passed through every phase and type of economy in its history. Originally a mining camp (called Hillyo for a short time), it was briefly a stop on the stage line as well as the Burlington Railroad. Logging was once a predominant source of income, supplanted now by tourism.

Field Note: I shot this view from the deck of a condominium built on the hillside about where the original photographer stood.

1890

"Write us at Custer, S.D."

Early modes of transportation and some of the fashions of the era are preserved in this view of the south side of Custer's Main Street. Note the construction activity on the brick building slightly left of center. Knowing that it was built in 1890 permits us to accurately date the photograph.

9-19-05 • N 43 45 57.4 W 103 36 01.7 • East

The building that dates the historic photo now houses the Custer County Chronicle. Brick has largely replaced wood on Custer's Main Street (also called Mt. Rushmore Road) and cars have replaced the horse and buggy.

Circa 1930
"Hermosa, S. Dak."

The Pioneer Town Site Company platted Hermosa in 1886 along the route of the Fremont, Elkhorn & Missouri Valley Railroad. For most of its life it has been a trading center for local ranches and farms. This was the way Hermosa appeared when President Calvin Coolidge showed up for a church service in 1927. The president vacationed in the Black Hills that year and attended the formal dedication of Mount Rushmore.

5-4-06 • Private Land • North

The foreground rail bed is still active, belonging to the Dakota, Minnesota & Eastern Railroad. Hermosa is now a growing bedroom community for Rapid City, a few miles north on Highway 79.

Field Note: As in other towns on the plains around the Black Hills, it is difficult to rephotograph Hermosa because there is no nearby hill providing an overview of the town's layout.

Circa 1895
"Court House, Parrot Hotel and Plunge Bath, Hot Springs, S.D."

The train is just rolling into town past the prominent Fall River County Courthouse, built in 1891, in this view of the north end of Hot Springs. Like others of his time, W.R. Cross was probably hired as a photographer by the railroad (which reached here in 1890) to shoot this advertising image on a special mount declaring the Black Hills to be "The Switzerland of America."

The Black Hills Yesterday & Today

8-11-04 • N 43 26 17.0 W 103 28 40.8 • Northwest

The Parrot Hotel is gone today, the courthouse has lost its cupola, and the old railroad bed lies beneath the pavement of North River Street. The Evans "Plunge Bath" is in the same place (upper right), but in a newer building. And homes now dot the ridge lines above town.

7-8-05 • N 43 26 15.7 W 103 29 45.6 • SOUTHEAST

1891
"Minnekata Ave., from Soldiers' Home"

Finished in 1890, the State Soldier's Home (facing page) was built of pink sandstone from a local quarry. It was the first substantial building made of stone in Hot Springs.

The Soldier's Home is now called the Michael J. Fitzmaurice South Dakota Veteran's Home. The main building still stands on the site (above), now surrounded by more recent construction and trees. The facility continues to be used as it was originally intended, providing services for South Dakota's military veterans.

Circa 1908

View from Soldiers' Home Looking Towards the Battle Mountain Sanitarium"

A cannon and a statue of Gen. John A. Logan, carved from sandstone by a local artist, frame the view in front of the former Soldiers' Home on the northwest edge of Hot Springs.

The Battle Mountain Sanitarium, in the distance, was completed in 1907 and became part of the Veterans Administration in 1930.

The Black Hills Yesterday & Today

5-8-06 • N 43 26 11.4 W 103 29 39.2 • East

The view across the valley is still pleasant today even though it is obscured by trees. The cannon has been replaced by a more modern version, but the statue of Gen. Logan hasn't moved from its spot across the street from the present-day Michael J. Fitzmaurice South Dakota Veteran's Home.

Field Note: The historic image (as well as the modern one) was taken from the second-floor veranda of the administration building.

Circa 1925
Hot Springs, S.D.

A number of early photographers used this vantage point, looking north down North River Street, to record the development of Hot Springs and the substantial, picturesque buildings that were erected in the business district. The castle-like Evans Hotel at right is a landmark of the town.

8-11-04 • PRIVATE LAND • NORTH

Many of the same buildings of native sandstone still stand along North River Street (which is also part of Highway 385), including the Evans, which now serves as housing for the elderly. Homes dating to the 1800s can also be seen atop the ridge above town. The railroad is gone, but the former depot is still in use (center left), and Fall River has been channeled between concrete walls.

Field Note: For more information about historic Hot Springs, be sure to visit the Fall River County Pioneer Museum nearby at 300 N. Chicago St.

Circa 1910
Waiting for the Train, Dewey, S.D.

Close to the Wyoming border in southwestern Custer County, Dewey was at one time a commercial center with stores and a post office (out of view to the right). It was also a shipping point on the Burlington Railroad, which arrived in 1890, for cattle from surrounding ranches. Here a crowd has gathered between the water tower and the depot, apparently awaiting the arrival of the next train.

6-15-05 • N 43 31 48.3 W 104 02 28.4 • NORTH

Today there is nothing left of the depot or the water tower except foundations in the gravel alongside the tracks. Foundations also mark the location of some of the commercial buildings, while others still stand, long-since abandoned. There are also one or two occupied homes and a church.

Field Note: Special thanks to Mary Hallenbeck, who helped me figure out the geography of Dewey during my visit there. I generally find that the smaller the town, the friendlier the folks, and certainly it was true here. The GPS reading is for the adjacent gravel road; stay off the tracks!

Oct. 18, 1894
"Edgemont, S.D. Irrigating Canal 14 Miles Long."

The Chicago, Burlington & Missouri Railroad reached this area in 1889, the year before Edgemont was established. The railroad has always been important here, and most of the buildings at upper right are near the rail line.

The irrigation canal promoted in this image was a feat of engineering but not a practical success. There was never enough water available to irrigate successfully.

6-15-05 • N 43 17 46.0 W 103 49 43.5 • NORTHEAST

The camera location is on a small rise on the southwest edge of town, near where the original high school stood long ago. The canal has now been filled in with soil, though remnants of it may possibly be visible here.

Field Note: As with other towns on the plains, luxuriant tree growth has obscured much of what you can see of the buildings and other landmarks. Without a high point nearby, this was the best available vantage point for a "birds-eye view".

8-29-05 • N 43 17 53.3 W 103 49 30.4 • NORTHEAST

April 25, 1903
President Roosevelt Visits Edgemont

President Theodore Roosevelt (facing page) drew an enthusiastic crowd in Edgemont on April 25, 1903, en route home to Washington from a hunting trip in Montana. Local history states that a group of cowboys (possibly those visible at right) lured the Rough Rider President to a chuckwagon supper, spoiling plans for a formal dinner prepared by the ladies of the town.

The newly restored band stand where Roosevelt spoke is now surrounded by green lawns and mature trees in Edgemont's city park.

Field Note: As far as I could tell, the recently restored gazebo has not been relocated since 1903. When you're here, be sure to visit the Trails, Rails and Pioneers Museum, which is right next to the park in downtown Edgemont.

Newcastle Wyo

The Black Hills Yesterday & Today

9-27-05 • Private land • Southwest

Circa 1900
"Newcastle, Wyo."

Named for its English counterpart, Newcastle was a relative late bloomer in the Black Hills region, founded when the Burlington Railroad reached the area in 1889. The historic view (facing page) is looking west down Main Street, with the original City Hall and fire station at left. What appears to be a sheepherder's wagon is parked beside a walkway.

The municipal building has disappeared in the modern view (above), which was taken from the front yard of a private home.

Circa 1930

"Main Street Newcastle, Wyo."

By the late 1920s or early 1930s, the Main Street of Newcastle was lined with businesses and automobiles. Note the old-style gas pump in front of the Chevrolet dealership at left.

The Black Hills Yesterday & Today

6-15-06 • N 43 51 15.5 W 104 12 20.5 • Northwest

The former Chevrolet dealership is perhaps the most recognizable of the buildings that still exist in the modern view, several others remain as well.

The Anna Miller Museum, off Highway 16 on the east side of town, offers exhibits and more information about the history of Newcastle and nearby Cambria.

Facing Page: 9-27-05 • N 44 24 30.5 W 104 22 46.0 • South

Circa 1895
Sundance, WY

Sundance Mountain looms above the town that bears its name. Starting life as a trading post in 1879, Sundance was incorporated as a city in 1887 — four months after a young horse thief named Harry Longabough was locked up there. Thenceforth he would of course be known as the Sundance Kid.

Sundance has grown into a mid-sized town (facing page), seen here in the fall. Note how thickly the trees have grown on the mountain in the past 100-plus years.

More information on the history of the area is available at the Crook County Museum, in the county courthouse, the yellow building at left center.

Seeing the Sights

In the waning years of the 19th Century, the Black Hills experienced another shift in travel patterns and eventually in its economy. No longer were people coming just to seek their fortune or to live a better life. Now they would come for a short while as visitors, seeing the sights and enjoying the natural beauty of the area.

Also by this time, with the invention of "dry" glass plate negatives and Kodak cameras using roll film, almost anyone could take photographs with relative ease. There are dozens of images of the "The Switzerland of America" (an early marketing slogan) taken by professionals who set up studios in the principal towns, some even advertising their offices in more than one city. Coming into vogue at the same time were black-paged, leather-covered albums full of amateur photos taken by camera-toting tourists. And it is still possible to find the quaint collections of images by Black Hills residents who recorded their corner of the world for posterity.

We also begin to see postcard views offered for sale to early tourists in the Hills, starting around 1906. Many of these images were black-and-white prints on postcard stock, printed one at a time by the photographer from the original negatives. Other postcards were commercially printed in color, usually in gaudy, artificial hues added by artists at the printing press, based on a black-and-white original photo. Often the reverse side of these postcards would carry a message to the folks back home, commenting on the beauty of the Black Hills, just as they do today.

These early tourism images portrayed nearly all the landmarks we know so well: Harney Peak, Devil's Tower, the Badlands, the Needles Highway, Custer State Park, Spearfish Canyon and Bear Butte. Some photos demonstrate a fascination with smaller-scale rock formations such as "The Traffic Cop" along the Needles Highway or the long-lost "Guardian of the Pools" somewhere near Sylvan Lake. A bit later there was tremendous interest in another rock formation after it was altered by a sculptor who added the faces of four presidents. As we visit these places today, we can reflect on those generations of earlier visitors who have enjoyed both the natural and man-made wonders of the Black Hills.

"Sylvan Lake on the B. & M. R.R."
8-1-04 • N 43 50 45.3 W 103 33 48.3 • Northwest
(Facing page, inset) In the 1890s and early 1900s, Sylvan Lake, northeast of Custer, was probably the most photographed tourist location in the Black Hills. Nearly every museum archive holds images such as this one, showing the graceful lodge completed in 1895 by Theodore Reder. The lake had formed behind a dam built across a natural cleft in the rock wall at the end of the former valley in 1892. The area's beauty, and its proximity to the Needles and Harney Peak, have made it a favorite stop for Black Hills visitors for well over 100 years. (Adams Museum & House/Locke)

(Facing page) The lodge burned down in 1935, but its location can still be seen in the grassy area along the shore at left. The rocks in the right foreground were submerged in the lake when the level of the dam was raised. Sylvan Lake is now part of Custer State Park, and still one of the prettiest sights to see in the Black Hills.

Field Note: *The historic image was shot from a rock outcropping that extends into the middle of the lake. If you look carefully, you will see the camera was leaning a bit to the right when the original photo was taken.*

(Below) Images from a 1929 Black Hills promotion. (Paul Horsted Collection)

Seeing the Sights: The Beautiful Black Hills

Circa 1925

Badlands Entrance Road Above Cedar Pass

There seems to be no problem with heavy traffic in this mid-1920s view taken along the track leading into Cedar Pass at the Badlands. A dog admires the scenery from the rear seat of the photographer's car.

The Black Hills Yesterday & Today

9-3-05 • N 43 45 33.0 W 101 56 10.6 • SOUTHWEST

Now paved for the thousands of vehicles that pass here each year, the highway has been straightened and re-routed. While some background formations remain much as they were in the 1920s, a large area has collapsed at upper left along the ridge line.

Field Note: I believe I was standing right on the camera site here. Note the little ridge running up to the camera from lower left in both views.

Circa 1930
"Cedar Pass — Hotel and Cabin Camp"

A fledgling tourist industry has taken root in the Badlands in this scene from an undated picture postcard, probably made about the time the park was authorized by Congress as a National Monument in 1929. It was officially given that status by President Franklin D. Roosevelt's proclamation ten years later.

South Dakota Senator Peter Norbeck, who had been a driving force in creating Custer State Park and Mt. Rushmore in the Black Hills, was also instrumental in establishing Badlands National Monument. He worked closely with Ben Millard, who with his sister Clara Jennings built and operated the facility seen above before the park was set aside.

Note that the original postcard image crops off some of the pointed spires at top.

5-4-06 • N 43 44 51.0 W 101 56 28.3 • NORTH

Where the cabins once stood is now the rear parking area for the newly-built Ben Reifel Visitor Center. While some peaks remain virtually unchanged in the background, others have slumped or disappeared entirely. A major collapse along this Badlands skyline was documented in the mid-1980s.

Out of view to the left is the present-day Cedar Pass Lodge, including a restaurant and cabins. It is possible that some of the cabins in the earlier photo are still in use at the new location. They were apparently moved when the highway was rerouted in this vicinity.

Field Note: The low ridge just visible in the middle ground, above the trucks at right, verifies this location. And if those cabins in the postcard are indeed still in use, they have been modernized and now provide a wonderful, rustic getaway that I have enjoyed on several visits.

Saddle Pass Cave, Interior, S.D. No. 6

5-4-06 • N 43 45 29.6 W 101 58 19.8 • North

Circa 1900
"Saddle Pass Cave, Interior, S.D."

"Saddle Pass Cave" is in a canyon east of the present-day Saddle Pass trail head along the Badlands Loop Road. This image (facing page) was taken by the photographer who shot "Big Foot Pass" (next page), probably on the same day around 1900.

The modern image reveals that little has changed in more than 100 years. The cave opening appears to be about the same size, and the peaks above seem to have weathered very little. Note, however, that the area of vegetation has grown considerably.

Circa 1900

"Big Foot Pass Near Interior, S.D."

A horse and buggy traverses the trail through Big Foot pass in the Badlands "wall" just a decade after the Sioux chief for whom the area is named traveled here with his people. Big Foot's band would later camp about 45 miles to the southwest, at a place called Wounded Knee Creek. An outbreak of fighting there on Dec. 29, 1890, led to the massacre of more than 250 Indian men, women and children by the U.S. Army.

5-4-06 • N 43 47 41.7 W 102 03 00.6 • North

This area is still known as Big Foot Pass, visible from the Highway 240 loop road through Badlands National Park. The photo site is a few hundred feet north of the road.

On the bluffs at left, the original trail has eroded into a gully; and the middle foreground has also changed.

The tragedy at Wounded Knee is commemorated each winter by the Big Foot Memorial Ride, which focuses on healing the wounds of the past. Riders on horseback follow the route used by their ancestors, celebrating and honoring the Lakota culture.

Seeing the Sights: The Beautiful Black Hills

5-4-06 • N 43 45 59.9 W 102 00 29.2 • EAST

Circa 1930
"A Parapet With A Nodule"

A fascinating example of erosion, this "parapet" consists of a sandstone boulder on top of softer Badlands sediments. At one time it was lying on a hillside that eroded away over a long period, leaving the rock sitting on top of a pinnacle that continues to shrink beneath the harder sandstone cap.

Field Note: This formation (also called a hoodoo or toadstool) is visible from the Badlands Loop Road, and I had photographed it in the past. I was delighted to be able to add it to this project when I found a historic postcard of the "parapet."

The Black Hills Yesterday & Today

10-8-04 • N 44 21 17.4 W 103 55 24.3 • WEST

Circa 1895
Falls and Logging Camp at Savoy, Spearfish Canyon

From the east rim of Spearfish Canyon, the view is of a logging camp established in 1890 just above Spearfish Falls (lower center part of the photo). The rail line crossed the head of the falls, continuing down the canyon at right. (See next page for a close-up of Spearfish Falls.)

Modern Savoy consists of Spearfish Canyon Lodge (left) and Latchstring Inn (right) along Highway 14A, which runs the length of Spearfish Canyon.

Field Note: I had several 1890s photos that were taken in this vicinity, but this was the one for which the modern view was least blocked by trees. It surprised me that even these overview images from the very rim of the canyon could be obstructed in this way.

213

Seeing the Sights: The Beautiful Black Hills

Circa 1895
"Spearfish Falls, on the B. & M. R.R., So. Dak."

Early fishermen in the creek below Spearfish Falls have an audience of tourists on a platform and excursion train above, where the rail line originally passed. The creek was diverted by Homestake Mining Company in 1916 to power a generating plant farther down the canyon, effectively shutting off the waterfall for 90 years.

8-8-04 • N 44 21 11.0 W 103 55 47.1 • SOUTHEAST

Now that the Homestake Mine has closed, the stream has been returned to its original bed and Spearfish Falls flows once again. Located just over the cliff below Latchstring Inn at Savoy, the Falls can be reached by a hiking trail. The area is only a few yards below the parking lot and highway, but seemingly in a world of its own.

Field Note: There are numerous early views of this waterfall from many angles, but this is one of the very few not presently blocked by tree growth. Pre-1890 images reveal that the falls originally separated into two or three channels that were combined into one when the rail line was built.

Circa 1910

"Latchstring Inn, In the Heart of Spearfish Canyon."

For some 90 years, Latchstring Inn (originally known as Glendoris) was a rustic stop for visitors to Spearfish Canyon. Tourists arrived by train in the early days, and later by auto. The lodge depicted in this hand-tinted postcard was torn down in 1989, to be replaced by a larger and more modern structure (facing page).

8-31-05 • N 44 21 11.4 W 103 55 54.6 • East

The original Latchstring Inn survives only in memory and historic photographs, but the modern facility is better suited to the volume of visitors who now come to Spearfish Canyon each year. The towering cliffs look much the same as they did 100 years ago, although they are gradually acquiring a coat of spruce and pine trees.

Facing Page: 8-8-04 • N 44 23 40.3 W 103 54 31.6 • Northeast

Circa 1900

"'Russell's Point' Spearfish Canyon"

Two men stand along the rails of the Burlington line below a landmark named "Russell's Point," a name not in common use today. Known as the Spearfish Branch, this line was built through the Canyon in 1893 and removed in 1933 after it was damaged by flooding. Much of the old railbed is now covered by Highway 14A, but it is still visible in some places beside the road.

Circa 1910
Fishermen in Spearfish Canyon

There was no caption information with this photograph of two anglers trying their luck in Spearfish Canyon. After a rail line was built in 1893, the train could drop visitors off in the Canyon each morning on the way from Deadwood to Spearfish, then pick them up on the way back later that day.

8-8-04 • N 44 22 23.1 W 103 55 08.0 • SOUTH

Spearfish Canyon today still attracts anglers and visitors who marvel at its beauty. The forest is regenerating here, gradually obscuring the view of the hills and the limestone cliffs in the distance.

Field Note: The artificial bank at right was constructed to keep the stream from eroding the highway, just out of sight at the top of the slope.

1899

D.C. Booth Fish Hatchery

Authorized by Congress in 1896 as the Spearfish station of the U.S. Commission of Fish and Fisheries (predecessor to the U.S. Fish and Wildlife Service), the Booth Fish Hatchery's mission was to produce and stock fish in the Black Hills. The hatchery building, shop, ice house and ponds were completed in July 1899, about the time of the arrival of D.C. Booth, the first hatchery superintendent. Dirt raceways in the foreground would be modernized with concrete raceways in the 1930s. These were in turn replaced in 1996, when the earlier concrete failed.

9-1-05 • N 44 28 51.8 W 103 51 38.5 • West

The original hatchery building, little changed in 106 years, is today used for administrative offices and a museum. The improved raceways are still rearing trout for the Black Hills through a cooperative effort with the State of South Dakota. The hatchery also protects and preserves fishery records, as well as artifacts for educational, research and historic purposes, and provides interpretive and educational programs for the public.

Field Note: The Booth Hatchery is highly recommended. The visitor center offers an amazing underwater fish-viewing aquarium kids will love.

Seeing the Sights: The Beautiful Black Hills

6-22-05 • N 44 23 51.9 W 103 45 32.1 • NORTH

July 4, 1919
Gen. Leonard Wood and Seth Bullock at Mt. Roosevel

Gen. Wood and Bullock stand in front of the newly-completed monument to Bullock's old friend, former President Theodore Roosevelt, who had died just months before. The monument was constructed by the Society of Black Hills Pioneers at the request of Bullock, a founding member of the group. Bullock himself died two months after this image was made. The tower and site were undergoing restoration at the time of the modern photo.

Field Note: This site is off the beaten path but not hard to get to from Deadwood, and you will likely have it to yourself. Turn left off Highway 85 on Mount Roosevelt Road, about a mile northwest of town. Two miles of twisting gravel road leads to the parking area, and a 10-minute hike brings you to the tower. Note that the tower itself is closed to visitors at this writing.

7-20-04 • N 43 53 33.6 W 103 32 52.3 • SOUTHEAST

Circa 1895
"Scene Showing Harney Peak in the Distance..."

In the historic view, dead and partially burned trees lie across a gap between sandstone cliffs that frame Harney Peak in the misty distance. Today, the Palmer Creek Road passes through the same opening. The road system in the area has been routed into a scenic loop with the result that no matter which way you are traveling, you pass through this gap with a view of Harney Peak in the distance.

Field Note: When I first laid eyes on this historic photo, I had a hunch the site would be found at this location. Some of the lower cliff formations were removed during road construction to widen the gap.

1933

Iron Mountain Road to Mt. Rushmore

The project of carving Mt. Rushmore (in distance at right) had strong support from South Dakota Senator Peter Norbeck, who had also been the primary force in establishing nearby Custer State Park almost a decade earlier. Norbeck and others foresaw the benefit of building a scenic highway between the park and the emerging mountain carving, and Iron Mountain Road was completed about 1927. Norbeck himself laid out much of the route on horseback and foot before the engineers started their work.

5-4-06 • N 43 52 06.0 W 103 26 06.3 • WEST

The Iron Mountain Road (now part of Highway 16A) today follows the course set for it by Norbeck some 80 years ago, though it has since been paved and made safer with the addition of guardrails. Norbeck suggested that the curving route should never be traveled at more than 20 miles an hour to appreciate the scenic beauty it passes through, still good advice today.

Field Note: Both the historic image and the new one were taken from above the northernmost tunnel, on the west side.

Seeing the Sights: The Beautiful Black Hills

Circa 1930

Pigtail Bridge, Iron Mountain Road

Another engineering marvel of the Iron Mountain Road is a series of "pigtail bridges" that achieve a maximum change in elevation while minimizing the grade and the space required. They were originally made of local logs to blend with the surrounding scenery. The hand-tinted historic image is a lantern slide, used in an early photo projection system.

5-4-05 • N 43 51 41.3 W 103 26 16.0 • NORTH

The pigtail bridges are still a delight, amazing visitors who travel between Custer State Park and Mt. Rushmore National Memorial. Upgraded in recent years to accommodate larger vehicles and heavier traffic, they still blend with the environment.

There are several trees common to both views, including the scarred veteran at left with the curved trunk. Note the stump at lower right, all that remains of the larger tree growing in the foreground of the historic image.

Circa 1925
Gutzon Borglum at Mt. Rushmore

Sculptor Gutzon Borglum ponders the still-uncarved Mt. Rushmore in this image that was probably taken around the time of the first dedication ceremony. An American flag, barely visible on a pole at upper left on the mountain, was planted during the ceremony on October 1, 1925. The image could have been taken as late as 1927, however, when the drillers first went to work.

5-4-05 • N 43 52 32.0 W 103 27 29.2 (Closed to Public) • Northwest

The completed carving gleams in the morning sun as a National Park Service ranger looks out from Borglum's former location. Only Washington and Lincoln are visible in this unusual angle, with Jefferson and Roosevelt tucked away between them. Borglum did not know in 1925 exactly where the final carvings would be made, or even all of the presidents who would be depicted.

Field Note: This site is on the grounds of Mt. Rushmore National Memorial, in an area not open to the general public. Intrigued by the unusual angle of Rushmore, years ago I had shot an earlier version of this view without knowing about the historic photo.

Seeing the Sights: The Beautiful Black Hills

FACING PAGE: 3-3-06 • N 43 52 40.7 W 103 27 18.1 • WEST

1928-29
Beginning Mt. Rushmore

Washington is just emerging in this early view of the carving. Progress at this stage was by no means continuous. Work would proceed until money ran out, then stop for months or even a year; virtually no progress was made during all of 1928. Additional Federal funding was made available in 1929, and the workers were called back. But money would continue to be an issue in the carving of Mt. Rushmore.

Field Note: These images were shot from the site of Borglum's original studio, the present-day Borglum View Terrace at Mt. Rushmore. He later built a larger studio nearby, which is still open as a museum. While you're here you will also want to visit the Lincoln Borglum Museum cleverly located beneath the main viewing terrace at Mt. Rushmore.

Circa 1930

Washington Emerging

A photograph much like this one, but without the scaffolding over George's face, is dated July 4, 1930. This image was presumably made a few months earlier, before work resumed. Note how little change is visible since the time of image on the preceding spread. Progress was very slow during Rushmore's first five years, mainly due to lack of funding. By 1930, however, Washington's eyes, nose and mouth had begun to appear, and the Father of Our Country was now recognizable.

3-3-06 • N 43 52 36.4 W 103 27 23.0 • Northwest

This location is just south of what is now the main viewing terrace at the monument. The Park Service utility building at lower left may have been built on the site where the camera was originally placed.

In the past, visitors couldn't get much closer to the mountain than this view, but the recently opened Presidential Trail offers a pleasant walk among the trees and several interesting perspectives on the sculpture.

Seeing the Sights: The Beautiful Black Hills

1933

Road Near Mt. Rushmore

Charles D'emery was a Connecticut-based photographer hired by Gutzon Borglum (and later the Park Service) to document the work on Mt. Rushmore. He took many outstanding images of the monument as well as the beauty of the surrounding Black Hills (found elsewhere in these pages). Here we see a car that appears in some of D'emery's other images, as well as a figure sitting on rocks at right, in front of the partially-carved mountain.

The Black Hills Yesterday & Today

3-3-06 • N 43 52 35.2 W 103 27 18.5 • NORTHWEST

The earlier image can be dated by the emerging image of Jefferson to the left of Washington. Inadequate rock in that area caused Borglum to remove the carving by 1934 and start over on the other side.

Today the former highway is the Avenue of Flags leading to the main viewing terrace at Mt. Rushmore. Note the same rock formation at right, with several feet of earth removed from around its base.

Field Note: I shot this location several times, trying to better match the alignment of the rock at right. The key was finally learning that the former road bed had been graded down during construction of the Avenue of Flags. I then used a ladder to regain the lost height, resulting in the image above. My wife Camille and daughter Anna Marie stroll toward the mountain early one late winter morning.

Seeing the Sights: The Beautiful Black Hills

Facing Page: 9-27-05 • N 43 52 35.9 W 103 27 28.7 (Closed to Public) • Northwest

1933

Jefferson and Washington

A hand-tinted lantern slide provides a comparison with Borglum's earlier effort, before Jefferson's likeness was removed. Here his nose and eye are visible to the left of Washington.

Seeing the Sights: The Beautiful Black Hills

7-31-04 • Private Land • Southwest

1925
"Keystone Cliffs and Old Rushmore"

In one of those unusual twists of history, the monument bears the name of a New York attorney who came to the Black Hills in 1885 to check on tin mining claims. When Charles Rushmore asked his guides for the name of a granite peak (facing page), they jestingly told him "Mount Rushmore." He later donated to the project.

Although the foreground area is now part of the town, "Old Keystone" is where the original mining camp was located in 1891. Note the helicopter near Mt. Rushmore in the distance (above), a common sight during the summer. The four-lane highway was built to handle the millions of visitors who travel to the Memorial each year.

Field Note: Both the modern and historic images were taken from the area of the Peerless Mine above Keystone.

Seeing the Sights: The Beautiful Black Hills

7-10-04 • N 43 52 41.8 W 103 27 16.1 • West

Oct. 1, 1925

"Senator Norbeck Speaking at Rushmore Dedication"

Senator Peter Norbeck, standing at right during the first dedication ceremony at the Memorial, had already done much for the Black Hills by the time of this photograph. After establishing Custer State Park and developing the Needles Highway, he had been attracted to State Historian Doane Robinson's vision for a massive sculpture.

It took much longer than anyone expected, and the Memorial was never truly "finished" according to Gutzon Borglum's design. But when the sculptor died at the same time that war clouds were gathering and financial support was drying up, work was stopped late in 1941.

The 1925 dedication was held near the site (left) where Borglum's main studio would later be built. The steps were also added at a later time.

5-4-05 • N 43 52 40.1 W 103 26 58.9 (May Be Closed to Public) • West

Circa 1935

"America's Greatest Monument"

Tourist traffic was on the rise by the mid-1930s, when the new likeness of Jefferson was well under way beside the emerging Lincoln and Roosevelt.

The old road bed (modern view at right) is now an overflow parking area and helicopter landing zone.

Seeing the Sights: The Beautiful Black Hills

Facing Page: 8-20-05 • N 43 50 53.9 W 103 32 11.9 • East

Circa 1920
"The Needles From Trail"

These grand spires are part of the group that appears in the 1875 image on page 28. The camera location is near present-day Trail 4, not far off the Needles Highway.

A brown area of insect-killed pine trees is visible in the center of the modern image. Part of a forest cycle, these dead spots have become more numerous in recent years and are more likely to spread through dense stands of timber like this one.

Field Note: In all my years of hiking around the Needles, Sylvan Lake and Harney Peak, I had somehow failed to note the section of Trail 4 that passes near these beautiful spires. It is highly recommended for a short hike to a gorgeous location.

Seeing the Sights: The Beautiful Black Hills

6-1-05 • N 43 50 29.8 W 103 32 43.6 • East

Circa 1930
"The Tunnel"

Originally known as the Crevasse Tunnel, this engineering marvel is 66 feet long and wide enough, after some modification (note that the large boulder at right has been trimmed considerably), that modern tour buses can just barely pass through — winning great admiration for their drivers each time the feat is accomplished.

The tree in the crevasse survives, but appears to be in decline today.

7-27-04 • N 43 50 29.2 W 103 32 39.4 • WEST

Circa 1925
"Tunnel Drive, Sylvan Lake, S.D."

The stereoview above shows the other (east) end of the Crevasse Tunnel on the opposite page. The unidentified individuals are probably family members of the photographer; they also appear in other views in the book.

In the modern image, hikers and automobiles sometimes share the busy tunnel during the height of the summer tourist season.

Seeing the Sights: The Beautiful Black Hills

Circa 1930

"Switchback on Needles Road"

The Needles Highway was laid out by Senator Peter Norbeck (later a supporter of Mt. Rushmore) with help from C.C. Gideon and civil engineer Scovel Johnson. Together they rode horseback and hiked through the formerly roadless area, gradually working out a route that was feasible for auto traffic and that still offers stunning views of the mountains, often framed by granite formations. The road was completed in the early 1920s.

In the postcard view above, the Cathedral Spires rise grandly above one of the hairpin turns for which the Needles Highway is now well known.

6-1-05 • N 43 50 26.5 W 103 32 07.2 • North

The original photographer placed his camera beside the road. It is now paved over, although the safe speed probably hasn't changed all that much. Aspen and pine trees grow in profusion in the middle of the hairpin turn.

Facing Page: 6-1-05 • N 43 50 31.9 W 103 32 12.2 • East

Circa 1925

"The Spike, on Needles Highway, South Dakota"

This prominent spire along a bend in the Needles Highway is also called "The Traffic Cop," "The Sentry," "Totem Pole" or "Paradise Peaks" (see next spread) in other early images.

Today tour buses have become an increasingly popular way for visitors to see the Hills in comfort while learning about the sights from experienced guides.

FACING PAGE: 8-20-05 • VICINITY N 43 50 33.1 W 103 32 13.3 • SOUTHEAST

Circa 1925
"Looking down on Paradise Peaks, Sylvan Lake"

This 1920s stereoview is the work of an energetic photographer named Loock, who climbed to a rocky crag high above the Needles Highway for this striking perspective.

The "Paradise Peaks" are virtually unchanged (facing page), although, as is true nearly everywhere else, a few more trees now grow around them — and from them.

Field Note: One of my favorite locations in the book, this was also one of the most difficult. I used a rope to safely reach the exact spot Loock used — the only one he *could* have used. His legs probably straddled the granite spire just as mine did, but I wonder if his were shaking, too! The GPS reading was recorded at a reasonably safe area nearby. Please do not climb to this location without proper safety gear.

Circa 1930
"View From Top of Big Tunnel in the Black Hills"

The title was a little misleading in the search for this location. The historic photograph was not taken from the top of the "Big Tunnel," but from a high rock about a mile east on the Needles Highway. Note the highway curving into the distance at center left.

8-20-05 • N 43 50 29.2 W 103 32 10.1 • SOUTHEAST

Note the way the tree at left has "popped up" in the past 75 years, while others have also grown up around the towering spires. The high point just left of center at the horizon is Mt. Coolidge, where several television and radio broadcasting towers are now visible on its summit.

Field Note: Climbing to this camera point requires a bit of caution. It appears that it may have been easier to get here in earlier times, but removal of some rock along the highway has now made it more of a challenge. The GPS coordinates are provided, but use care if you venture here.

Circa 1933
Black Hills Winter Sports Club Carnival

Although there was no information on this image, *Custer County Chronicle* articles of the early 1930s mention a ski jump and annual winter carnival at Silver Tip Hill near Sylvan Lake (in Custer State Park), and this would appear to be the place. The unidentified ski jumper is flying past a crowd of several dozen spectators, while other people wait below around bonfires and parked Model A cars. A lack of reliable snowfall in the Southern Black Hills led to the end of the winter carnival by 1936.

1-14-06 • N 43 50 32.0 W 103 34 40.0 • NORTHEAST

According to Custer State Park personnel, this area was cleared of trees in recent years and used to skid logs down to waiting trucks, one reason it is still largely "open" after 70 years. Sylvan Lake is just over the hill to the left, and Harney Peak is visible in the distance at top.

1891

"Lake Harney Peaks"

Two young ladies pose in a wooded glen below towering granite rocks in this scenic view. The photographer's title "Lake Harney Peaks" has not been found on any other documents or maps of the era. It presumably refers to a lake that was already forming, or soon would be, behind a dam under construction in 1891, off camera to the left. The area was called also "Custer Lake" about this time but eventually acquired its present name, Sylvan Lake.

The Black Hills Yesterday & Today

7-31-04 • N 43 50 43.7 W 103 33 51.4 • Northwest

The original camera point is today under several feet of water. This image was taken from the shore of Sylvan Lake in approximate alignment with the original photo site. Note the couple in a small boat paddling near the rocks at left.

Field Note: I am sure that some of the tourists who were walking by at the moment I found this location wondered what I was so excited about. Based on the caption supplied by Grabill I had guessed that these rocks would be found near Sylvan Lake, but I didn't expect to find them *in* the lake.

Circa 1895 and 1902
Sylvan Lake

These three images, two historic and one modern, were all taken from the same high point east of Sylvan Lake. The stereoview above (left pane) was shot just after completion of the lodge on the far shore, before the gazebo was added. The hand-tinted image on the facing page — with gazebo now in place — was made about 1902, when photographer William Henry Jackson is known to have visited the Black Hills.

Given the many beautiful locations around the lake, it is a curious coincidence that both photographers would have chosen this relatively obscure position.

Circa 1930

"Sylvan Lake, Black Hills, So. Dak."

The photographer caught the morning mist rolling through the valley in this image made above Sylvan Lake at sunrise. The beautiful lodge on the opposite shore was finished in 1895 and burned down in 1935.

Note that the gazebo or pavilion at right has been moved from its position in an earlier image on the preceding page.

5-12-06 • N 43 50 50.3 W 103 33 44.3 • WEST

There is still a road down to the site of the lodge, but where the road ran beside the lake is now a foot path. No sign remains of the lodge itself, or the gazebo, more than 70 years after the fire. A new Sylvan Lake Lodge was opened in 1937 on the ridge off camera to the left, and is still serving visitors to this part of Custer State Park.

Field Note: There is no more beautiful place in the Black Hills than Sylvan Lake at sunrise on a quiet spring morning.

Seeing the Sights: The Beautiful Black Hills

1922

Camping at Sylvan Lake

The year of this photo can be seen under magnification on the license plate of the Model T at left. Several people cook their breakfast over a campfire on the shore of Sylvan Lake in a scene from a hand-tinted glass lantern slide, apparently part of a set created by the Forest Service to promote the Black Hills.

8-1-04 • N 43 50 47.2 W 103 33 45.7 • SOUTHEAST

In the modern photo, a beach now lines the north shore of the lake where the campers once cooked. At the height of summer, the cool (some would say cold) waters of this mountain lake attract locals as well as visitors from outside the Black Hills.

No. 167. Wedge Rock. Scene in Custer Park on the B. & M. R. R., 6 miles from Custer.

Circa 1900

"Wedge Rock"

Wedge Rock was a natural attraction near Sylvan Lake, depicted in a number of early photographs. These visitors are not identified, but given their finery it is quite possible that they had strolled the few hundred yards from their vacation quarters at Sylvan Lake Lodge.

5-12-06 • N 43 50 53.1 W 103 34 06.1 • WEST

The surprising colors visible in the modern image of "Wedge Rock" are caused by variations in the granite as well as lichen growing on the surface.

Hikers and rock climbers still use this area, but there seem to be fewer visitors who make it a destination now that the "old" nearby Sylvan Lake Lodge is gone.

Field Note: Reaching the photo site requires some agility in climbing onto a boulder (partially seen at lower left) at least the size of "Wedge Rock."

Seeing the Sights: The Beautiful Black Hills

5-5-06 • N 43 51 58.7 W 103 31 55.6 • SOUTH

Circa 1895
Harney Peak Spires

Two early rock climbers venture onto a spire near the summit of Harney Peak in this 1890s stereoview taken by Quiggle & Johnson, photographers from Rapid City.

Very little has changed at this elevation in 110 years. The same crystals of granite and even the same lichen are visible in both images.

The back of the Cathedral Spires and parts of Custer State Park are visible in the distance.

Field Note: I had guessed that this site was in the Needles area, but otherwise had no idea where to find it. One day, while working on other historic images on Harney Peak, I noticed this cleft beautifully framing the Cathedral Spires, and thought I might take a photo of it. Then I realized the foreground spires looked familiar. When I pulled out a reference copy of the historic image, I knew I had stumbled onto the location.

8-22-05 • N 43 51 56.6 W 103 31 51.6 • NORTH

August, 1920
Harney Peak Fire Tower

This seems to be the first fire tower on Harney Peak. Compare it with the one on the following spread, which has five windows on a side instead of three. Guy wires kept the tower from blowing away during mountain storms.

The tower in the present-day image was built by the Civilian Conservation Corps in 1939 on the site of the earlier two towers, but this time of native stone. Note the right foreground rocks in both images.

Circa 1930
"Harney Peak, Black Hills, S.D."

This is the second Harney Peak fire tower, built in the 1920s. The cabin at lower right served hikers as well as those who arrived by burro, which was another way to reach the top in the early days. The spire at far right is the "summit" shown in an 1875 image on page 33.

8-22-05 • N 43 51 57.1 W 103 31 56.2 • East

The present-day tower on Harney Peak dates to 1939. It is no longer staffed as a fire tower but is a popular destination for hikers in the Black Elk Wilderness Area.

Harney Peak is the highest point in South Dakota, and also noted as the highest point east of the Rocky Mountains.

Circa 1930

"Needles From Harney Peak"

An early picture postcard depicts an unidentified hiker gazing from Harney Peak toward the distant Cathedral Spires in Custer State Park. The granite of the Harney Range was part of the igneous intrusion that swelled up beneath layers of rock deposited by an ancient ocean, forming the Black Hills.

5-5-06 • N 43 51 56.6 W 103 31 57.7 • SOUTH

The layers of limestone and sandstone that once buried Harney Peak have eroded away over a period of 60 million years. But granite changes very little in the split second of 75 years, and the rock formations visible in the modern photo are virtually identical in appearance to those in the historic image.

Field Note: This location is a few hundred feet west of the fire tower on the summit of Harney.

Seeing the Sights: The Beautiful Black Hills

3   LODGE IN CUSTER STATE PARK, BLACK HILLS, S. D.   91194

Circa 1925

"Lodge in Custer State Park, Black Hills, S.D."

The State Game Lodge, as it is now commonly known, was built in 1920 and later served as the "Summer White House" for President Calvin Coolidge in 1927. President Dwight Eisenhower also stayed here in 1953.

6-6-05 • N 43 45 50.5 W 103 22 48.8 • Northwest

The Game Lodge has been expanded in recent times with wings of additional rooms on either side, but it still preserves the rustic feeling of another era when the president enjoyed fishing in nearby Grace Coolidge Creek, which had been renamed for his wife.

Field Note: Just up the road from the Game Lodge is the Peter Norbeck Visitor Center, with a fine museum and interpretive displays about the natural and man-made history of Custer State Park.

8-6-05 • N 43 41 09.4 W 103 35 19.9 • East

Circa 1900
"Beecher's Monument, 120 ft. high, near Custer, S.D."

"Beecher's Monument" is a pair of pillars to the east of present-day Highway 385 about five miles south of Custer. They are a curiosity in this part of the hills, well away from the spires and towers of granite closer to Harney Peak. Much larger than they seem in photos, the rocks are visible from miles away in certain directions.

Gen. Custer recorded a visit to these formations in August 1874, and they were named "Turk's Head" on a map of the Black Hills produced following his expedition. From another angle, they do look like a head wrapped in a turban. Locally they are now generally referred to as Beecher Rock or Rocks.

How "Beecher's Monument" got its name remains uncertain, however. The name appears on maps as early as 1884, so it may be the name of an early "discoverer" or a homesteader in the area. Some say it was named for the famous preacher, Henry Ward Beecher.

The Black Hills Yesterday & Today

10-20-05 • N 43 48 31.6 W 103 36 47.4 • NORTH

Circa 1895
Crazy Horse Memorial

There is no title attached to the glass plate negative from which the historic image was made. But it is, at this writing, the oldest known image of the mountain that would later become Crazy Horse Memorial, seen in the new image following a blast during the carving process.

Sculptor Korczak Ziolkowksi started carving the mountain in 1948. Although he died in 1982, his wife Ruth and their family continue to guide the work on this impressive mountain sculpture that commemorates the spirit of the famous Lakota Sioux leader and his people.

Field Note: The historic image was taken at some distance from Crazy Horse, so this is one of the few examples in the book where I cropped the original to show a distant object. If you are in the Custer area, do not miss a visit to Crazy Horse Memorial, where a large visitor center includes a museum, interpretive displays, a theater, and Native American crafts and artwork for sale.

Seeing the Sights: The Beautiful Black Hills

Circa 1895
"Wind Cave, S.D."

These are some of the earliest buildings, including a hotel (the large building), near the original entrance to Wind Cave during an era when it was operated as a private tourist attraction. Following a dispute between the partners who had claims on the property, the federal government withdrew the land from homesteading in 1899, saying no party had established a homestead or pursued any mining. Wind Cave National Park was then established in 1903.

The Black Hills Yesterday & Today

7-8-05 • N 43 33 30.7 W 103 28 45.8 • South

The original, natural entrance to the cave is out of view at lower right. An interpretive walking trail loops through the area today, while visitors gain access through a man-made entrance a few hundred feet away, descending into the cave with the help of an elevator. A visitor center is located off camera to the left, up the trail.

Field Note: I believe this image is within 20 feet of the original site; there aren't many clues here except the known original entrance to the cave in the canyon below.

Circa 1925
"Buildings at Wind Cave National Park"

The buildings in the previous historic image had been replaced by a newer facility (behind the cars at center) when this picture postcard was produced in the late 1920s. A landscaped sign created from white-washed rocks in 1919 advertises the cave, while the statue and grave site of Alvin McDonald (next historic photo) can be seen in the distance at left.

7-8-05 • N 43 33 28.4 W 103 28 51.3 • East

The foreground building appears to be the one in the old postcard, now modified with additions. Today it is used as the fire office for the park. The sign on the far hillside disappeared in 1928, when the National Park Service directed the superintendent to remove it. He merely turned over the white-washed rocks, which are still there. Careful examination of both images reveals that small saplings on the far hillside have now grown to mature pines.

Circa 1925
Statue of Alvin McDonald

Alvin McDonald was not the "discoverer" of Wind Cave, but he was one of the first to know it well. In 1890, at age 18, he began exploring the depths of the cave (originally a mining claim managed by his father), creating a field notebook now on display at present-day Wind Cave National Park visitor center. McDonald's work was cut short when he died of typhoid fever in 1893 following a trip to Chicago's Columbia Exposition, where he helped publicize the cave. It has been speculated that his illness may have stemmed from the hundreds if not thousands of hours he spent in the cave.

McDonald was buried at this site just above the entrance to the cave he loved.

7-8-05 • N 43 33 29.6 W 103 28 45.3 • Southeast

The grave site is marked today by a bronze plaque mounted on a stone (placed in 1959), summarizing McDonald's achievements. The statue was removed at some unknown date decades in the past, and a search for it is now underway by the Park Service at Wind Cave. Note the present size of the once-small lilac bush over the grave.

Circa 1930

"Beaver Creek Bridge"

Built in 1929 for more suitable access to the newly developing Custer State Park, the Beaver Creek Bridge spans one of two perennial streams that flow into Wind Cave National Park. The builders were able to create the illusion that the underlying arches rise naturally from the rock walls on either side of the canyon. It is the only bridge in the state using this type of arch.

The Black Hills Yesterday & Today

7-8-05 • N 43 35 05.1 W 103 29 20.6 • SOUTH

The bridge is two miles north of the present-day Wind Cave visitor center on Highway 87, and is also visible from a pullout near the Centennial Trail head. The road bed is 115 feet above the canyon floor.

Circa 1895
Chautauqua Grounds

A Chautauqua program was organized by prominent Southern Hills citizens as an annual series of educational lectures (in the building at left) in Hot Brook Canyon near Hot Springs. Here the crowd is lining up for food being prepared at a central table.

7-8-05 • N 43 26 39.9 W 103 29 15.3 • SOUTHEAST

The site of the Chautauqua grounds, witness to so many large gatherings, is today a peaceful, out-of-the-way city park on the northern outskirts of Hot Springs. If you wish to visit the photo site itself, the easiest access to the cliff top is through nearby Evergreen Cemetery.

1892
"Crystal Lake and Marble Point, Rapid City, South Dakota"

It appears to have been a cold day when this promotional photo was taken at "Crystal Lake." Ice still covered much of the water, and the stiff-looking model is no doubt trying to stay warm while holding still for the long exposure required by the photographic technology of the 1890s. Like all lakes in the Black Hills, Crystal Lake was formed by damming a stream, in this case Rapid Creek.

The Black Hills Yesterday & Today

8-17-05 • N 44 03 31.6 W 103 17 21.3 • SOUTHWEST

Crystal Lake is known today as Canyon Lake, and Marble Point is now a tree-covered ridge. The lake is a jewel of Rapid City's parks system that has been renovated several times over the past century, notably after the disastrous 1972 flood and again in more recent years, when fishing piers and other visitor-friendly features were added.

Field Note: This site presented a challenge, because the prominent cliff in the old photo seemed to be missing. I finally noticed the tree-covered hill and, from another angle, saw some of the rock features visible in the historic photo. That allowed me to work my way to the approximate location of the original camera site.

Seeing the Sights: The Beautiful Black Hills

1890
"Devil's Tower and Mo. Buttes... 2 Miles from Camera to Tower."

Devil's Tower, which would become the United States' first national monument in 1906, is a striking presence in this Wyoming landscape of newly fenced pastures. The surrounding ranches were still fairly recent in an area that had been settled only in the previous 15 years. An irrigation ditch crosses the middle foreground.

"Mo. Buttes" are the lesser-known Missouri Buttes on the horizon at far right.

9-28-05 • PRIVATE LAND • SOUTHWEST

A beautiful fall day accents the colors of the landscape and the cottonwood trees on the plains below the tower. A highway now crosses the former pasture (possibly following an old road barely visible in the historic image). The irrigation canal was dry when this photo was taken.

Field Note: This view may be observed from Highway 24 (crossing near the center of the photo) just northeast of Devil's Tower.

1890

"Devil's Tower"

These pools are along the former bed of the Belle Fourche River, probably in late summer when flows would have been reduced. The Arapaho, Crow, Cheyenne and Lakota Sioux all have their own legends that describe the creation of the tower, generally involving a giant bear clawing his way toward seven girls stranded on a patch of ground being lifted by the gods.

Scientists would call it a laccolith, an intrusion of igneous rock beneath layers of sedimentary material that has since eroded away.

The Black Hills Yesterday & Today

5-25-05 • Private Land • West

The re-routed Belle Fourche River now runs along the base of the hill in the middle distance, while nearly full-grown trees stand in its old bed. A fence line still marks the boundary between private property (on this side) and the National Monument. Controlled burns on the slopes around Devil's Tower have recently reduced the number of trees that had grown up there in the past 115 years.

Field Note: The camera site was on a high bank of the old river bed, though that cannot be seen here.

Paul Horsted's Project Notes

Gathering the historic photos and preparing for fieldwork

As noted in the introduction, the scope of this project grew and evolved, almost of its own accord, far beyond the limits I had originally imagined. After a year or so of advance work and research, I established the following criteria for selecting historic images for use in this book.

1. The original photograph should have been taken between 1874 and about 1935, in part to allow for early photos of the carving of Mt. Rushmore (starting about 1927), a subject that has always fascinated me. On the other hand, the vast quantity of historic photos becomes overwhelming after 1935, as photography became a hobby for millions of people. It was a fair date with which to end.

2. Generally, the selected historic photo should be a landscape, rather than a narrow view of a single building or a portrait of a person. Some exceptions were made for particularly significant buildings, like the State Game Lodge in Custer State Park.

3. The photograph should have been taken within the geographic area defined here as the Black Hills region, roughly bounded by Newcastle, Sundance and Devil's Tower on the west; Edgemont and Hot Springs on the south; Badlands National Park on the east; and Bear Butte, Newell and Belle Fourche on the north.

I tried to visit almost every public archive or museum in the region (please see the list of more than 50 collections consulted on page 301). I also called on several private individuals, some of whom have collections rivaling those at any museum in the state. Without exception, I was welcomed and given access to review photographic archives that varied in size from a few prints of one small town to literally thousands of historic photos taken by dozens of pioneer photographers.

Some collections had a searchable database or listing of subject matter. In others it was necessary to review every photo in box after box. During this process I looked at a minimum of 75,000 images to gather the nearly 1,800 views considered for use in this project. Many of the photos I quickly bypassed were obviously of no use for a rephotography project: portraits of people, interiors of buildings, or nondescript landscape images such as cows in a field, with no clue to location noted on the photograph. But interesting, potentially identifiable landscape shots and views of towns and other landmarks were scanned on-site into my laptop computer.

The process of working with historic photos continued in my office at my home north of Custer. There I made backup copies of the original digital scans. Then I cataloged each image, adding "metadata" to record what collection the photo came from; what pertinent information, if any, was written on the front or back of the original photograph; and who the photographer was, if known.

Sadly, only a fraction of historic photographs, usually those made by professionals, carry the photographer's names, which is why many of the images in this book display the unsatisfying credit line "photographer unknown." Also, very few images carry a date or even a year. Thus, many photos are dated here as, say, "circa 1895." Clues to dating photos included knowing when a certain photographer operated here; whether or not any automobiles, trains or tracks are visible; dates of construction (or destruction, by fire or development) of certain key buildings (courthouses, schools) in various towns; and to some extent the style of photography or the type of material on which the photo was printed.

Preparing for fieldwork, I printed an 8-by-10 reference photo of each image and inserted these into an ever-growing set of albums, divided by towns and regions of the Black Hills. These were all placed in a box in my car, always available whenever I traveled the area. At any time I could pull whatever album was needed, find the images of, say, Sturgis, and begin my search for photo sites.

The ideal historic photograph for this project was a clear, well-exposed and well-preserved image of a known town or site, with the photographer's name imprinted on the front. If I was lucky, a year or even a precise date would appear on the back. With a reference copy of such an image in hand, I could go to the town or general location and start trying to figure out the point from which the image had been taken. When I found a location, I could learn whether it

Setting up the camera for a shot at the site shown on page 245. (Paul Horsted photo)

was possible to place my camera where the earlier image was made and make a meaningful comparison photograph.

And that, it turned out, was the big question: Was it possible to make a modern matching photo at each location?

How the historic photo sites were located

In doing slide presentations about this project over the past several years, the number one question has been: "How did you find all these places?" The answer is twofold: with help from knowledgeable people around the Black Hills; and with more than three years of searching by car and on foot. Some sites (such as an image of early Mt. Rushmore) are fairly easy to narrow down, although not as easy as they might seem at first. One image of the mountain carving in progress (see page 236, with old car on highway) took three visits and about six hours of searching the grounds before I realized that a rock on the right side of the photo was the same one now visible along the Avenue of Flags. Until that moment I had been convinced that the image was along the present-day Presidential Trail, which also follows part of the old roadbed. Even after finding the location, I returned two more times, trying to achieve a closer match with the historic photo. Eventually this meant setting up a ladder to regain the ten feet of height lost when the small hill where the camera originally stood was graded flat during later construction of facilities and sidewalks. (The site is within six feet of the southwest front door of the restaurant at Mt. Rushmore.)

Other photo sites took much, much longer to find. There are eight images in this book that were taken in the wilderness around the summit of Harney Peak, for example. I spent days hiking around up there (including seven trips to the top), sometimes off the marked trails, and I still haven't found all the sites I was hunting for. Harney Peak is well-represented in this book, however, including the first-ever pictures taken there in 1875.

When I could, I would try to find someone at the local museum in each town (perhaps while I was scanning photographs there), or maybe someone downtown on Main Street, who could look at an obscure (to me) old photo and say, "That looks like Pluma, the north end of Deadwood along Highway 385." This kind of assistance saved me many hours of work, and I'm very grateful for help from "local experts" across the Black Hills. In particular, Dr. David Wolff of Black Hills State University oriented me to the "historic geography" of the northern Black Hills mining districts.

Among the easiest sites to find, at least to begin with, are those in known towns or cities. Once I stood somewhere above the town with the reference image in hand, I could get an idea which way the streets and buildings were oriented, and perhaps identify hills or landforms that could guide me to the precise location. In the Black Hills, early photographers tended to use the highest points available to shoot photos overlooking towns; once I realized this, I would always begin by looking for the tallest hill near a town. But there was still a learning curve; once I established an orientation to the geography, I could start to zero in on specific locations.

In some cases it appeared from a distance that a photo site was on private property, requiring contact with the landowner before venturing in to find out. For example, I had several early (1876-1880) views of Bear Butte I was eager to track down. By driving around the butte I established that most of them were taken from the west or northwest, in one or two large pastures. Eventually I was able to locate the landowners and obtain permission to hike across their property to find the sites.

When I explained what I was trying to accomplish, literally every single landowner I contacted gave me full permission to operate on his or her property. Most were quite interested to learn that Black Hills history was documented in or from their back yards or pastures. The names of these kind folks are listed in the acknowledgments, and I want to again express my gratitude for their help.

What I eventually learned about searching for historic photo sites is that if you can "find the background" of the photo (distant mountain tops or other large background landscape features), you can often work your way to the foreground. But not always. Sometimes the foreground is so absolutely changed, or hidden in trees that block the distant reference points, that it's not possible to pinpoint where the earlier photographer placed the tripod, even though you know you're within a few yards.

I also maintained a file of compelling but completely unknown locations. These were images that seemed to show a Black Hills site (perhaps

Reviewing reference photo for the site on page 205. (Paul Horsted photo)

taken by a photographer who I knew had done other work here) but which carried absolutely no information about their location. Because their content or composition was so interesting, I continued to hope that I could somehow track them down. (A good example of one I did find is on page 11). I would file these away in the back of the reference book (and the back of my mind) and work on them as time permitted. I still have a few of these "unknown" images on file, and perhaps will include those in a future book — if I can find them!

Re-photographing historic photo sites

As I learned in our earlier book, *Exploring with Custer,* locating a historic photo site and actually rephotographing it well are two entirely different tasks. There remains the technical and creative challenge of setting up the camera at the right angle, with a lens of the right focal length, to replicate the historic photograph as closely as possible. Sometimes it's very difficult to tell if you are indeed at the right location, and I would never claim to be at the precise location of every image in this book.

Looking at the images published here, I estimate that I was within three feet of 30 percent of the original photo sites; within 10 feet of 50 percent; and within 300 feet (possibly farther) of the remaining 20 percent. The last category includes those images for which the site cannot be determined exactly, perhaps due to a lack of definitive objects in the foreground, or where the site has been obliterated by mining, road building, construction or other factors, as explained in the captions.

Consider a place above Deadwood known as McGovern Hill, behind the present-day Slime Plant. The photographer arrives in, say, 1883, takes a photo, and moves on. I arrive 122 years later. In the intervening years, the hillside has been logged, homes have been built on it and then removed, and a large ore-milling operation has operated there for some 80 years. (I can see all these things in various historic photos). There is now a railroad bed cut into the steep hillside, and a huge flat space carved out where tanks for the city water supply have been constructed. I find a place that reasonably matches the 1883 camera site. Some of the same buildings are still visible in the town below, and the same distant mountains as well. The view looks "right," but is it the "exact same location" the photographer stood upon? Does that place even exist any more? I don't know.

See page 51 and judge for yourself.

At the other extreme was one of my visits to the top of Harney Peak, looking for the site of a stereoview image from around 1895. I finally saw the same granite spires as in the background of the image, and arrived about where I thought the camera point should be. Lo and behold, sticking out of the granite in front of me were the same little pieces of quartz that are visible in the historic photo, still there after 120 years, and I knew I was putting the tripod legs almost exactly where photographers Quiggle & Johnson did so long ago. That is exciting! (See page 268.)

As seen in this example, determining the precise location where a historic image was taken (within three feet or less) is only possible when the original photographer composed his image with a rock formation, unusual tree or surviving building near the camera point. In some images, however, the nearest foreground "clue" is hundreds of yards away, making the same level of precision impossible.

In either case, once I found the general location, and agreed with myself that it was the site, I would set up my camera and begin trying to solve several more potential mysteries. Was a tripod used? If so, where was it placed? How high was the camera? Was it a few feet this way or the other way? Especially fun were a few sites where I found a flat rock or other inviting level space close by. Virtually every early photographer used a tripod, so such a solid flat surface would almost certainly be the place he put it. At times, that was where all elements in the photo would come together, and I'd find I was at exactly the right location. (See page 40 for an example of where this happened.)

Even after finding the right location, I sometimes encountered a dilemma. If the view from the photo site was now blocked by trees, should I move a few feet away? The right answer for me, most of the time, was "yes." I could see no point in multiple modern photos of tree trunks when a clearer view of the landscape was available a short distance away.

As often as possible, I tried to shoot the modern photo at the time of "discovery," when I first realized I had found the site. Working with hundreds of images, this was a necessity, especially for locations that were hard to reach. Accordingly, I chose not to place an emphasis

Checking a location above Sylvan Lake. (Steve Wilson photo)

on trying to match the time of year or time of day, especially since we do not know the date or even the year for many of these historic images. If the light was "wrong" (coming into the lens, for example, or obscured by clouds), I would try to schedule a second visit to a location. In many cases, however, I was able to match the lighting by waiting an hour or two for the sun to shift or clouds to part.

The one remaining issue before I made my shot was determining the focal length of the lens used by a particular photographer. Careful study of the historic images usually revealed whether a wide-angle or "normal" lens had been used, but the precise focal length was an unknown. When possible, I used clues such as the arrangement of elements in the picture (like rocks or buildings). Then a zoom lens could be adjusted to match what I saw in the historic photo.

The cameras and technology used for making pictures from 1874 to 1935 could be the subject of an entire book, but a brief introduction will have to do here. The earliest photographers in the Black Hills used the "wet plate process." This involved coating a piece of clean glass with liquid chemicals immediately before exposing it through the camera lens (or two lenses if shooting in stereo). Exposures would run from five to thirty seconds, after which the glass plate would be developed in a nearby dark tent. It was a very cumbersome process, but in the hands of a master such as Illingworth or Morrow, the quality and clarity of detail in the resulting images is still astonishing after 130 years. By the early 1900s, "dry plate" negatives and celluloid film made photography a much easier process, and we see many more photos taken during this period. Even amateurs were starting to record their lives and travels. By the 1920s and '30s, Kodak and other camera manufacturers had brought photography to the masses, and the variety of images from this period is even greater.

My own camera gear included Kodak Pro 14n, Fuji S2 and Nikon D70s digital cameras, 17-35mm and 28-70mm zoom lenses, Gitzo tripod, Garmin GPS unit, and a backpack to carry it all. Almost as important in this digital era was the hardware back at my office. The digital photos were processed (and this book designed) on Macintosh G4 and G5 computers, and proofed on Epson printers.

The technology of photography continues to evolve rapidly, of course. I shot *Exploring with Custer* almost entirely on film, and this book, just five years later, was done solely with digital cameras. I'm sure the equipment used for this project will seem as outdated someday as the 1870s "wet plate" cameras look to us today, but I'm quite proud of the results. I only hope the digital formats available at the moment will survive as well as those glass-plate negatives and stereoviews have done during the past 130 years!

Changes and similarities at the historic photo sites

As hinted elsewhere, the single most obvious change at the majority of historic Black Hills photo sites is the tremendous growth of Ponderosa pine trees. If you choose 50 historic landscape photographs taken here before 1935, you may find that only 10 of them can be rephotographed successfully. The others are partially or completely blocked by trees. The older the historic image, the more likely this is true. At many locations I knew I was standing precisely where the historic photo had been taken, but was stymied by a present-day view of tree trunks and pine boughs blocking the formerly open, panoramic view. This phenomenon (which echoes what we found while working with the Custer Expedition images) is seen around every one of the towns I visited in the Black Hills region. The growth, or over-growth, of trees is also found at places like Spearfish Canyon, Devil's Tower, Harney Peak, Needles Highway, and on the plains around the Hills.

As the project continued, it became almost a surprise to find a historic photo site that was not blocked by trees. I have included enough modern examples of "tree trunk" photos to make the point, but I regret the many fascinating historic images left out of this book simply because a modern photo of tree branches or trunks, taken from the historic position, is not very compelling or informative. Be sure to note that in many of the modern-day images in this book, trees are just starting to grow into the foreground. In a few years these sites too will be blocked

Tree-blocked site near Pringle; see page 41. (W.H. Over Museum)

Project Notes/Bibliography

by trees, unless there is thinning, a prescribed burn or a forest fire.

The reason for this particular environmental change is quite simple. Since the days of settlement in the Black Hills, we've done a pretty good job of suppressing fires — both natural (from lightning) and man-made — which used to burn through this area and thin out the downed timber and smaller Ponderosa pine trees. The result of more than 100 years of fire suppression is a much denser forest, one where smaller trees are growing closer together, and one that is increasingly prone to catastrophic forest fires as the fuel builds up year after year.

The over-growth of Ponderosa pine has other, less obvious ramifications for the environment, such as reduced flow of water into our streams and aquifers, as well as reduction in wildlife populations and species diversification. It's a very subtle, gradual change that has taken more than a lifetime to develop. We're not very good at perceiving these types of slow changes from day to day, but the historic photos give us a chance to see exactly what is going on over time.

In addition to trees blocking many sites, another perplexing issue arose when the land or hillside the historic photographer stood on was simply "gone" or transformed into something else. When a highway is widened again and again over time, from a two-track stagecoach trail to a four-lane superhighway, hundreds of yards of hillside — the one where the 1800s photographer stood — can simply disappear (page 57). And when an open cut mine expands over time to swallow up entire mountains and the towns built on them (as well as photo sites within the towns), it is very difficult to position the camera properly.

Historic images taken in a town, as opposed to a hilltop overlooking the town, could also prove to be a challenge. Deadwood in 1876 is shown in many photos, but re-shooting the actual site for some of them would require standing inside a building or pointing the camera at a brick wall in a back alley (if I could even figure out where the location was). In these photos, there is no apparent relationship between what was and what is today, nothing to tie "then and now" together. Naturally, I found this very disappointing. The 1870s image looks so solid, so "real," it is hard to accept that the scene has faded completely into oblivion.

Self-portrait, roof of Butte County Courthouse in Belle Fourche. See page 123.

But half the fun of a project like this is trying to figure it all out. If all history mysteries were resolved, the world — and the Black Hills — would be a much less interesting place!

If you don't see your town or favorite area in this book, it means I either didn't find enough historic photos of it, or the ones I did find didn't "work" well for this project because of the changes mentioned above. If you know of images you think should be included in a possible future expansion of this project, please refer to the contact information on page 2 and let me know.

My quest to find and rephotograph sites for this book continued right up to the publication deadline. In all, I visited about 300 sites and rephotographed about 200 of these. Some 160 of the best images are included here. These, and others that didn't make it into the book, can also be found on our web site, www.dakotaphoto.com. If you have questions or suggestions, please contact me through the web site. I would love to hear from you.

—P.H.

Bibliography

Clark, Badger. *When Hot Springs Was a Pup*. Hermosa, SD: Lame Johnny Press, 1983.

Curl, Barney. *Looking Back at Edgemont*. Self-published, 1984.

Douda, Joseph R. *Iron Ponies and Steel Rails of the Black Hills*. Unpublished manuscript.

Fielder, Mildred. *Railroads of the Black Hills*. New York: Bonanza Books 1964.

Fite, Gilbert C. *Mount Rushmore*. Keystone, SD: Mount Rushmore History Association, 1980.

Grafe, Ernest, and Horsted, Paul. *Exploring with Custer: the 1874 Black Hills Expedition*. Custer, SD: Golden Valley Press, 2002.

Gries, John Paul. *Roadside Geology of South Dakota*. Missoula: Mountain Press Publishing Company, 1996.

Hedren, Paul L. *With Crook in the Black Hills: Stanley J. Morrow's 1876 Photographic Legacy*. Boulder: Pruett Publishing Company, 1985.

Hesnard, Douglas B., ed. *Hermosa 1886-1986: Railroads, Cowboys and Memories*. Hermosa, SD: Hermosa Centennial Committee, 1986.

Higbee, Paul and Aney, Kathleen. *Spearfish, SD: A History*. Spearfish: Black Hills and Bighorns History Project, 2000.

Horsted, Paul. *Custer State Park: From the Mountains to Plains*. Custer, SD: Golden Valley Press, 2004.

Hurt, Wesley R., and Lass, William E. *Frontier Photographer: Stanley J. Morrow's Dakota Years*. University of Nebraska Press and University of South Dakota, 1956.

Kime, Wayne R., ed. *The Black Hills Journals of Colonel Richard Irving Dodge*. Norman, OK: University of Oklahoma Press, 1996.

Klock, Irma H. *Yesterday's Gold Camps and Mines in the Northern Black Hills*. Lead, SD: Seaton Publishing Company, 1975.

Kolbe, Robert, and Bade, Brian. *They Captured the Moment: Dakota's Photographers 1853-1920*. Sioux Falls, SD: Pine Hill Press, 2006.

Lee, Bob (Robert). *The Black Hills After Custer*. Virginia Beach, VA: The Donning Company, 1997.

_____. *Fort Meade & the Black Hills*. Lincoln, NE: University of Nebraska Press, 1991.

Mautz, Carl. *Biographies of Western Photographers A Reference Guide to Photographers Working in the 19th Century American West*. Nevada City, CA: Carl Mautz Publishing, 1997.

McLaird, James D. *Calamity Jane: The Woman and the Legend*. Norman, OK: University of Oklahoma Press, 2005.

Miller, David B. *Gateway to the Hills: An Illustrated History of Rapid City*. Northridge, CA: Windsor Publications Inc., 1985.

Mills, Rick W. *125 Years of Black Hills Railroading*. Hermosa and Hill City, SD: Battle Creek Publishing Co. and Black Hills Central Railroad, 2004.

Parker, Watson. *Deadwood: The Golden Years*. Lincoln, NE: University of Nebraska Press, 1981.

_____, and Lambert, Hugh K. *Black Hills Ghost Towns*. Athens, OH: University of Ohio Press, 1974.

Patera, Alan H., Gallagher, John S., and Stach, Kenneth W. *South Dakota Post Offices*. Lake Grove, OR: The Depot, 1990.

Shaff, Howard, and Shaff, Audrey Karl. *Six Wars at a Time*. Sioux Falls, SD: The Center for Western Studies, 1985.

Shuler, Jay. *A Revelation Called the Badlands: Building a National Park, 1909-1939*. Interior, SD: Badlands Natural History Association, 1989.

Strain, David E. *Black Hills Hay Camp: Images and Perspectives of Early Rapid City*. Rapid City, SD: Dakota West Books and Fenske Printing Inc., 1989.

Sundstrom, Jessie Y., ed. *Custer County History to 1976*. Custer, SD: Custer County Historical Society, 1977.

_____. *Pioneers and Custer State Park: A History of Custer State Park and North-Central Custer County*. Custer: Self-published, 1994.

Tallent, Annie D. *The Black Hills; Or Last Hunting Grounds of the Dakotahs*. Sioux Falls, SD: Brevet Press, 1974. (Reprint of the 1899 edition.)

_____. *The First White Woman in the Black Hills, as told by herself*. Mitchell, SD: Educator Supply Company, 1923.

Toms, Donald D., Schillinger, Kristie L., and Stone, William J., eds. *The Gold Belt Cities: The City of Mills*. Lead, SD: Black Hills Mining Museum, 1993.

Turchen, Lesta V., and McLaird, James D. *The Black Hills Expedition of 1875*. Mitchell, SD: Dakota Wesleyan University Press, 1975.

Twomey, Katherine, and Magee, Helen, eds. *Early Hot Springs*. Hot Springs, SD: A Star Publication, 1983.

Wolfe, Mark S. *Boots on Bricks: A Walking Tour of Downtown Deadwood*. Deadwood, SD: Dakota Graphics 1996.

In addition to traditionally published sources, several National Park Service web sites were consulted for historical information, as were other carefully selected on-line resources. Chief among these was Google Earth, a satellite photo browser at www.earth.google.com. that was used to verify GPS data collected at photo sites.

Acknowledgments

I could never have completed this book without the help of dozens of individuals and organizations across the Black Hills. I will forever be indebted to these folks who helped me in so many ways. To all, thank you for helping to make this book a reality.

In particular, I want to thank my wife, Camille, for her outstanding design work, which turned a merely interesting idea into a work of art. Although I get my name on the cover, this book is really as much hers as mine. Thanks also to our daughter Anna Marie for brightening each day in our home office and for understanding (at age four) why "Daddy can't play right now;" to Dr. David Wolff for his vast knowledge of Black Hills history, willingly shared; and to my great friend Ernie Grafe for coming in at the end, making my ramblings more coherent, and helping us pull it all together as the book went to press.

Special thanks also to my parents, Burt & Gladys Horsted, for their support of my projects, hopes and aspirations for forty-some years.

To the landowners or lessees I contacted during this project, all of whom gave me permission to search for photo sites on their property, my thanks: John & Nancy Gausman; Betty Gould; Ogden Driskill; Johna Rovere; Perry Livingston; George Whalen; Vic & Donna Fondy; Sandy Williamson; Steve Cullum; Ron Decker; Mechelle & David Powers; Leonard & Oonagh Wood; Scott Cameron & Denise Hanisch; Bob & Mary Regan; Bob Wicka; Mary Hallenbeck; Jim & Donna Willson; Betty & Ray Rumney; Duffy Buresh; Nita Atwood; Harvey Keene; Terry Torgerson; Hank Pepin; City of Deadwood; Cathy Jones; Merle & Arlene Harp; City of Newell; Bob Pesek; Gerry Eckert.

To the business owners or managers, who let me roam their property, climb on their roofs, et cetera, thank you also: Guido Della Vecchia and Johanna Meier, Black Hills Passion Play, Spearfish; Meg Warder, 1880 Train/Black Hills Central Railroad, Hill City; Tim Conrad, Dungeon Bar and Rushmore Office Supplies, Sturgis; Elaine Jensen, Butte County Courthouse, Belle Fourche; Tom's T's, Sturgis; Dale & Susan Berg, Berg Jewelry, Deadwood; Franklin Hotel, Deadwood; Alan Johnson, Palmer Gulch Resort/Mt. Rushmore KOA, Hill City; Ken Springs, Ken's Minerals & Trading Post, Custer; Randi Sue Smith, D.C. Booth Historic Fish Hatchery, Spearfish; Laura Pankratz, Borglum Historical Center, Keystone; Star Village, Rapid City; Trinity Lutheran Church, Rapid City; Custer Senior Center; Ken's Camper Sales, Lead; Steve & Kathie Ice, Deadwood KOA.

Additional historical research assistance from: Reid Riner, Minnilusa Pioneer Museum (at The Journey), Rapid City; Mary Kopco, Jerry Bryant, Ivan Hovland, Milton Miller, Arlette Hansen and Carol Reif, Adams Museum and House, Deadwood; Roberta Sago, Case Library, Black Hills State University, Spearfish; Linda Velder, Newell; Robert Kolbe, Sioux Falls; Brian Bade, Storyteller West, Rapid City; Harry Thompson, Center for Western Studies, Sioux Falls; Marcia Murphey, 1881 Courthouse Museum, Custer; Bruce Weisman, Mt. Rushmore National Memorial, Keystone; Dorothy Neuhaus and Shirley Anderson, W.H. Over Museum, Vermillion; Pat Roseland, Rapid City; Rick Mills, Hermosa; James & Peg Aplan, Antiques & Art, Piedmont; Blaine Cook, Black Hills National Forest; Charles Carlson, Black Hills National Forest Visitor Center at Lake Pactola; Brad Block, Custer State Park; Ruth Ziolkowski, Crazy Horse Memorial, Custer; Jim Pisarowicz, Wind Cave National Park; Michelle Ramos, Crook County Museum & Art Gallery, Sundance, WY; Peggy Sanders, Oral, S.D.; Anne Cassens and John Koller, Edgemont Trails, Trains and Pioneers Museum; Jessie Y. Sundstrom, Custer; Dorothy Honadel, Spearfish; Mike Runge, City of Deadwood Archives; Charles Rambow, Ft. Meade Cavalry Museum, Sturgis; Bob Hayes, Keystone Area Historical Society; Laurie Langland, Dakota Wesleyan University, Mitchell; Bobbi Jo Tysdal, Anna Miller Museum, Newcastle, WY; Dave Strain, DakotaWest Books, Rapid City; Donna Neal, Devereaux Library Archives, Rapid City; Linda Byrum, Edgemont Public Library; Helen (Reder) Daughenbaugh, Rapid City; Gerry Evans, Hermosa; Laurie Bozzetti, Rapid City; Milo Dailey, Belle Fourche; Charles D'emery, Oceanport, NJ.

Additional technical assistance and help finding photo sites: Mike Pflaum, Mt. Rushmore National Memorial; Scott Brown, Jim Cheatham and Christine Czazasty, Devil's Tower National Monument; Jason Fisher and Karl Burke, Homestake Mining Company; Bill Goehring; Steven Wilson; Jim Laverick; John Graf; Midge Johnston, Badlands Natural History Association; Herb & Jan Conn; Larry Shaffer and Robert Farrar, Black Hills Institute of Geological Research; Kevin Hachmeister, Crazy Horse Memorial; Mitchell Riner and Terri Riner; Custer County Search & Rescue.

Pollock & Boyden logo. (Brian Bade Collection)

Additional thanks: Sage Creek Grille, Custer; A Walk in the Woods Gallery & Gifts, Custer; Surroundings, Custer; ArtForms Gallery, Hill City; Darrel Nelson, Adams Museum & House; Steve Baldwin, Black Hills Parks & Forests Association; Johnny Sundby; Ray Summers and Joan Hunter, The Journey Museum, Rapid City; Tim Velder, Lawrence County Journal, Deadwood; Kevin Van Patten and Saturnino Eka John, South Dakota Public Television (Dakota Life program), Vermillion; Anne Ziolkowski, Crazy Horse Memorial, Custer; Charley & Norma Najacht, Custer County Chronicle, Custer.

Proofreading by: Kris Hachmeister, Dorothea Edgington, Reid Riner, Al Riner.

Even more help from: Hannah Schaup, Sam Hosman, Allison Hosman, Victoria Dahlstrom, Kaysha Cameron.

Inspiration and an appreciated look over my shoulder: Watson Parker.

And extra special thanks to Jon and Joanne Nelson for their encouragement and friendship, and for helping me appreciate what lies beneath.

Photographic Collections

The historic photos in this book were found within the following 50 collections. Not every collection's images are actually represented in these pages, but all have my equal thanks for their assistance.

South Dakota
1881 Courthouse Museum, Custer
Adams Museum & House, Inc., Deadwood
James & Peg Aplan, Antiques & Art, Piedmont
Brian Bade, Storyteller West, Rapid City
Black Hills Institute of Geological Research, Hill City
Case Library, Black Hills State University, Spearfish
Center for Western Studies, Augustana College, Sioux Falls
City of Deadwood Archives
Custer State Park, Custer
Corinne Darrow, Custer
D.C. Booth Fish Hatchery, Spearfish
Devereaux Library Archives, S.D. School of Mines & Technology
Edgemont City Library, Edgemont
Kevin Eilbeck, Rapid City
Fall River County Pioneer Museum, Hot Springs
Robert Farrar, Hill City
Fort Meade Museum, Fort Meade
Thomas D. Griffith, TDG Communications, Deadwood
Dorothy Honadel, Spearfish
Paul Horsted, Dakota Photographic LLC, Custer
Jessie Y. Sundstrom Historical Files, Custer
Keystone Area Historical Society, Keystone
Robert Kolbe, Sioux Falls
Layne Library, Dakota Wesleyan University, Mitchell
Daniel McPherson, Custer
Milton Miller, Belle Fourche
Richard Miller, Custer
Rick Mills, Rapid City
Minnilusa Historical Association, Rapid City
National Park Service, Mt. Rushmore, Keystone
Larry Ness, Yankton
Newell Museum, Newell
Don Pyn, Hill City
Pat Roseland, Rapid City
JoAnn Sanders, Caputa
Peggy Sanders, Oral
South Dakota State Historical Society, Pierre
Spearfish Area Historical Society (Joe Hargraves Collection), Spearfish
Dave Strain, DakotaWest Books, Rapid City
Tri-State Museum, Belle Fourche
United States Forest Service, Custer
W.H. Over Museum, Vermillion
David Wolff, Spearfish

Wyoming
Anna Miller Museum, Newcastle
Crook County Museum, Sundance
Wyoming State Archives, Cheyenne

Other States
Paul Hedren, O'Neill, Neb.
Fred McCartney, Chadron, Neb.
Troy L. Parker and James Parker, Rochester Hills, Mich.
Don Schwarck, South Lyon, Mich.
Library of Congress, Washington, D.C.

The antiques shown on the chapter opening pages are courtesy the Minnilusa Pioneer Museum and the 1881 Courthouse Museum.

Index

A

Adams Museum 2, 5, 9, 11, 37, 46, 50, 51, 54, 56, 58, 60, 62, 65, 66, 77, 78, 82, 90, 92, 94, 95, 98, 100, 101, 104, 108, 110, 134, 142, 144, 146, 148, 202, 214, 218, 224, 301
Allison, William C. 3, 276, 277, 301
America Center Road 19, 24
Anna Miller Museum 116, 118, 195, 196, 197, 198, 300, 301

B

Badlands 9, 10, 202, 204, 206, 207, 209, 210, 211, 212, 294, 299, 300
Battle Mountain Sanitarium 184
Bear Butte 20, 44, 79, 101, 105, 106, 107, 202, 294, 295
Bear Lodge 34
Bear Rock 94
Beaver Creek Bridge 284
Beecher's Monument 276
Belle Fourche 9, 10, 123, 125, 126, 128, 292, 293, 294, 298, 300, 301
Belle Fourche Dam 127
Belle Fourche rodeo grounds 122
Benecke 14, 26
Big Foot Pass 209, 210, 211
Bishop, A.L. 2, 3
Black Hills Illustrated 6
Black Hills Mining Men's Association 6
Black Hills National Forest Visitor Center 151, 300
Bloody Knife 23
Booth, D.C. 222
Borglum, Gutzon 6, 230, 231, 232, 236, 237, 238, 242, 300
Boulder Canyon 57
Boyden 3, 11, 51, 60, 61, 65, 101, 296
Brennan, John R. 110
Brown Rocks 50, 143
Buckhorn Mountain 86, 87, 91
Buckhorn Range 22
Buffalo Gap 41, 298
Bullock, Seth 224
Burlington & Missouri River Railroad 54, 72, 86, 87, 88, 156, 175, 188, 190, 195
Butcher & Son 3, 176
Butte County Courthouse 122, 125, 298, 300

C

Calamity Peak 20, 22, 24, 38
Cambria 44, 116, 117, 118, 119, 197
Camp Bradley 34
Camp J.G. Sturgis 101
Canedy, 3, 172, 206, 212, 262, 270
Canyon Lake 289
Castle Creek Valley 14, 15, 16, 17
Cathedral Spires 28, 30, 248, 268, 272
Cedar Pass 204, 206
Cedar Pass Lodge 207
Centennial Prairie 50
Centennial Trail head 285
Central City 62, 65, 68
Chase, Elda 109
Chase, Geo. 109
Cheyenne River 18
Chicago & N.W. line 140
Chicago, Burlington & Quincy Railroad 154
Chicago's Columbia Exposition 282
City Springs 110
Civilian Conservation Corps 269
Clarke 3, 209, 210
Collins, William J. 3, 112, 213, 220
Columbus Consolidated Mill 62
Comanche 104, 105
Coolidge, President Calvin 178, 274
Coules & McBride 3, 78, 104, 144
Cowboy Hill 158, 159, 160
Crazy Horse 36
Crazy Horse Memorial 22, 173, 277, 300, 301
Crevasse Tunnel 246, 247
Crook 13, 37, 38, 39, 40, 41, 94, 296, 299
Crook, General 6
Crook City 9, 14, 44, 76, 77, 150
Crook County Museum 198, 300, 301
Cross, William Richard 3, 114, 168, 180, 184, 278, 302
Crouch Line 115, 150
Crow Peak 135
Crystal Lake 288, 289
Custer 2, 13, 14, 16, 18, 21, 26, 28, 30, 33, 34, 36, 37, 38, 39, 40, 44, 80, 81, 82, 85, 86, 88, 93, 94, 100, 101, 104, 121, 176, 188, 276, 277, 296, 299
Custer's Trail 9, 27
Custer County Chronicle 177, 256
Custer County Courthouse 90, 91, 92
Custer Expedition 5, 6, 7, 9, 10, 17, 18, 20, 22, 23, 43, 80, 90, 297
Custer Lake 258
Custer State Park 202, 206, 226, 229, 242, 256, 257, 263, 268, 272, 274, 275, 284, 294, 300, 301, 304
Cyanide 9, 44, 74, 75

D

D.C. Booth Fish Hatchery 222
D'emery, Charles 3, 204, 226, 228, 230, 232, 236, 238, 240, 302
Dakota, Minnesota & Eastern Railroad 179
Dakota Territory 115
Darrow, Lewis 3, 188, 301
Deadwood 5, 6, 9, 44, 46, 47, 48, 49, 50, 51, 53, 54, 56, 57, 58, 59, 60, 61, 80, 86, 88, 121, 136, 138, 140, 141, 142, 144, 146, 148, 149, 220, 224, 295, 296, 298, 299, 300, 301
Deerfield 17, 100
Deerfield Lake 16
Devil's Tower 9, 10, 30, 34, 202, 290, 291, 292, 293, 294, 297, 300
Dewey 188, 189
Dodge 5, 6, 13, 299
Dodge-Newton-Jenney Expedition 6, 14, 24, 26, 27, 28, 29, 30, 32, 33, 34, 36

E

Eastman 3, 288
Edgemont 10, 18, 190, 193, 294, 299, 300, 301
Eisenhower, President Dwight 274
Elkhorn Mountain 11, 32
Ellison hoist 70
Elmore 72, 73
Ernest Grafe 2, 7, 9, 14
Etta Tin Mine 96
Evans, Fred 112
Evans Hotel 186
Evans Transportation Line 112

F

Fall River 95, 186, 187, 278, 286, 301
Fall River County Courthouse 180
Father DeSmet 65
Fellows, Harvey 136
Fey, Justus 3, 109
Fort Laramie Treaty 14
Fremont, Elkhorn & Missouri Valley Railroad 62, 78, 140, 178
French Creek 14, 18, 19, 20, 26, 27, 36, 38, 40, 43
Ft. Meade 44, 101, 102, 104, 106, 107, 300, 301
Ft. Meade Cavalry Museum 105, 164, 166, 300

G

Gayville 62, 64, 65
Gideon, C.C. 248
Gitchell, Dan 109
Glendoris 216
Goddess of Justice 122
Golden Reward 146
Gold Mountain Range 22
Gold Run Creek 44
Gold Run Gulch 54
Gordon 27, 36, 37, 40, 43
Grabill, J.C.H. 3, 6, 53, 88, 183, 258, 259, 290, 292, 302
Grace Coolidge Creek 275
Grafe, Ernest 2, 7, 9, 14, 299, 300, 302
Grizzly Gulch fire 53
Guardian of the Pools 202
Guerin, A (or Fritz W.) 3, 6, 14, 24, 26, 27, 28, 29, 30, 32, 33, 34, 36, 302

H

Hangman's Hill 110, 111, 160
Harney, Hank 44
Harney's Pass 29
Harney Peak 10, 11, 20, 28, 33, 88, 91, 100, 158, 202, 225, 244, 257, 268, 269, 270, 271, 272, 273, 276, 295, 296, 297
Harney Peak Tin Company 170, 171
Hawkins, B.E. 3, 81
Haxby, Orpha L. 109
Haynes, Frederick J. 3, 128, 302
Hermosa 178, 179, 299, 300
Hill City 43, 44, 80, 81, 100, 152, 170, 171, 172, 173, 174, 175, 299, 300, 301
Hillyo 175
Hollister 3, 274
Holy Terror Mine 98, 99
Homestake 6, 44, 55, 63, 65, 66, 68, 69, 70, 71, 214, 215, 300
Horsted, Paul 1, 2, 7, 10, 14, 209, 210, 212, 244, 247, 248, 262, 270, 274, 299, 300, 301, 303
Hot Brook Canyon 286
Hot Springs 10, 44, 95, 180, 183, 184, 186, 282, 286, 287, 294, 299, 301

I

Illingworth, William Henry 3, 6, 7, 9, 14, 16, 17, 18, 20, 21, 22, 23, 26, 297
Ingleside 144, 145
Inyan Kara 34
Iron Mountain Road 226, 227, 228

J

Jackson, William Henry 3, 134, 135, 260
Jefferson 231, 237, 238, 243
Jennings, Clara 206
Johnson, J. Harlan 3, 150, 152, 154, 156, 158, 268, 269, 300
Johnson, Scovel 248
Journey Museum 110, 301

K

Keystone 10, 44, 96, 98, 99, 240, 299, 300, 301
Korn, Sgt. 104

L

Lake Harney Peaks 258
Lakota Sioux 14, 17, 277, 292
Latchstring Inn 213, 215, 216, 217
Lead 6, 44, 54, 55, 62, 66, 69, 70, 72, 149, 299, 300
Lease 3, 248
Leedy, Carl H. 110
Lewis, Mattie 109
Lewis, Wm. 109
Lime Stone Peak 16
Lincoln 231, 243, 299
Little Big Horn 14, 19, 44, 101, 104
Locke & McBride 2, 3, 54, 266
Locke & Peterson 3, 116, 148, 214, 225
Logan, Gen. John A. 184
Longabough, Harry 198
Loock 3, 246, 252, 303
Lookout Mountain 133, 136
Ludlow, Capt. William 23

M

Manville, C.B. 3, 59
Marble, L.W. 3, 260, 288, 289, 303
Marble Point 288, 289
Mayberry, T.H. 3, 198
McBride, C.C. 2, 3, 54, 78, 104, 144, 266
McDonald, Alvin 280, 282
McGillycuddy, Valentine T. 33, 36
McGovern Hill 48, 146, 148, 296
M Hill 109, 113, 159
Michael J. Fitzmaurice South Dakota Veteran's Home 183, 185
Mickelson Trail 55, 87, 89, 100, 154, 157
Millard, Ben 206
Minnilusa Pioneer Museum 2, 6, 16, 17, 22, 23, 74, 86, 111, 115, 150, 152, 154, 156, 158, 162, 238, 256, 269, 284, 288, 300
Missouri Buttes 290
Monument Rock 96, 97
Moosecamp Lodge 150
Morrow, Stanley J. 3, 6, 9, 14, 37, 38, 39, 40, 41, 44, 48, 49, 58, 77, 82, 94, 108, 296, 297, 299, 303
Mt. Coolidge 255
Mt. Moriah 60, 61, 138, 140, 144
Mt. Roosevelt 224
Mt. Rushmore 44, 99, 109, 161, 173, 177, 206, 226, 229, 230, 231, 232, 236, 237, 240, 243, 248, 294, 295, 300, 301
Mystic 115, 150

N

Needles 6, 20, 91, 202, 242, 244, 248, 250, 252, 254, 268, 272, 297
Newcastle 117, 195, 196, 197, 294, 300, 301
Newell 9, 131, 294, 300, 301
Newell Museum 128, 129, 130
Newton Fork 100
Noonan, Pvt. 23
Norbeck, Senator Peter 206, 226, 242, 248

O

O'Neill Photo Co. 3, 174, 280, 282
Orman Dam 127, 128, 130
Owl Creek 128

P

Pactola 44, 150, 151, 152, 300
Palmer Creek Road 225
Palmer Gulch 11, 300
Paradise Peaks 250, 252
Parrot Hotel 180
Passion Play 133
Pennington County 152
Perkins, W.B. 3, 66, 303
Pigtail Bridge 228
Pike, J.W. 3
Pioneer Townsite Company 78
Pluma 54, 55, 295
Plunge Bath 180
Pollock 3, 11, 51, 60, 61, 65, 95, 100, 101, 296
Prairie Edge building 162
Presidential Trail 235, 295
Pringle 14, 41, 297

Q

Quiggle 3, 268

R

Ragged Top Mountain 74, 75
Rapid City 44, 108, 109, 110, 111, 112, 113, 114, 115, 150, 151, 160, 162, 179, 268, 288, 289, 299, 300, 301
Rapid City Indian Hospital 159
Rapid City Indian School 158
Rapid Creek 44, 109, 111, 112, 151, 158, 159, 288
Reder, Odo 85
Reder, Theodore 202
Reder Sawmill 85
Rise Studio 3, 127, 178, 242, 252, 254, 272
Robinson, Doane 242
Rochford 14, 154, 156, 157
Roosevelt, President Franklin D. 206
Roosevelt, President Theodore 193, 224, 231, 243
Rushmore, Charles 240
Russell's Point 218

S

Saddle Pass Cave 209
Saddle Pass trail 209
Savoy 75, 213, 215
Sentry 250
Sheridan 43, 152, 153
Silver Tip Hill 256
Skyline Drive 111
Society of Black Hills Pioneers 224
Spearfish 2, 44, 50, 56, 59, 74, 132, 133, 134, 135, 136, 137, 138, 214, 215, 222, 299, 300, 301
Spearfish Canyon 7, 9, 10, 72, 75, 202, 213, 216, 217, 218, 220, 221, 297
Spring Creek 43, 152
St. Onge 298
Standby Mine 156, 157
State Game Lodge 274, 294
State Soldier's Home 183
Stewart, Dr. R.A. 95
Stiff, C.W. 64
Stimson 6
Stockade Lake 37, 40, 296
Stockmen's Day 162
Stokes, George 110
Sturgis 44, 57, 59, 102, 105, 134, 164, 165, 166, 167, 168, 294, 300
Sturgis, Col. Samuel D. 101
Sundance 9, 10, 198, 294, 300, 301
Sundance Mountain 198
Sylvan Lake 5, 9, 10, 85, 202, 244, 246, 252, 256, 257, 258, 259, 260, 262, 263, 264, 266, 267, 296

T

Tallent, Annie 95
Terraville 62, 63
Terry Peak 75, 146
Traffic Cop 202
Troy 64, 300, 301

U

Union Pacific Railroad 6

V

Veteran's Administration hospital 105

W

Wall 9
Warren Lamb Lumber Company 158
Washington 70, 193, 231, 232, 234, 237, 238, 301
Wedge Rock 266, 267
Wharf Resources 63, 146
White Rocks 58, 59, 138, 144, 146
Whitewood 44, 58, 76, 78, 142
Whitewood Creek 46, 51, 61, 143
Wind Cave 278, 280, 282, 283, 284, 285, 300
Wood, Gen. Leonard 224
Wounded Knee Creek 210
Wyoming 2, 30, 116, 188, 290, 301

Y

Yates Hoist 55, 69

Z

Ziolkowksi, Korczak 277
Ziolkowksi, Ruth 278

We hope you enjoyed The Black Hills Yesterday & Today.

If you love the Black Hills, you may also enjoy these books published by Golden Valley Press. Available at www.dakotaphoto.com or at your favorite bookseller.

Exploring With Custer: The 1874 Black Hills Expedition
by Ernest Grafe & Paul Horsted. 8.5 x 11 inches, 300 pages in full color.
ISBN 0-9718053-1-8 (soft cover $34.95), ISBN 0-9718053-0-X (hard cover $59.95)

A uniquely intimate portrait of this fascinating Expedition emerges from the *first* photographs ever taken in the Black Hills, carefully matched with present-day images. The experience of the trail comes alive in the blend of photographs with personal diaries, newspaper stories and official reports. Maps and GPS coordinates also pinpoint dozens of locations visited, described or photographed in 1874. More information at www.custertrail.com.

Custer State Park: From the Mountains to the Plains
by Paul Horsted, 8.5 x 11 inches, 96 pages in full color.
ISBN 0-9718053-2-6 (hard cover, $19.95)

Custer State Park's 71,000 acres encompass a vast landscape of towering granite peaks, pine-covered mountains, sparkling lakes, and flower-strewn prairies. The Park is home to abundant wildlife, including one of the world's largest bison herds, and its natural beauty attracts more than a million visitors each year. Join photographer Paul Horsted on a scenic tour of this "Jewel of the Black Hills" as you explore Custer State Park through stunning nature photographs created over a period of nearly 20 years. Samples from the book at www.dakotaphoto.com.